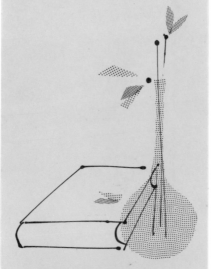

a gift...

saint paul public library

from the publisher

Twayne's United States Authors Series

Sylvia E. Bowman, *Editor*

INDIANA UNIVERSITY

Oliver Wendell Holmes

OLIVER WENDELL HOLMES

by Miriam Rossiter Small

Wells College

 29

Twayne Publishers, Inc.   ::   New York

SPECIAL LIBRARY EDITION PRODUCED BY
GROSSET & DUNLAP · *Publishers*
NEW YORK

Copyright © 1962 by Twayne Publishers, Inc.

Library of Congress Catalog Card Number: 62-19473

MANUFACTURED IN THE UNITED STATES OF AMERICA BY
UNITED PRINTING SERVICES, INC.
NEW HAVEN, CONN.

To
Bertha Bartlett Small,
who can remember waiting on Beacon Street
in 1893 to see Dr. Holmes emerge
for his morning walk

Preface

BECAUSE the Autocrat became a public image which Dr. Oliver Wendell Holmes enjoyed and lived up to, there has been little looking behind the image he made so personal, so wise, and so humorously winning. Passing years have now made possible a needed search behind the image: to distinguish the influence of the eighteenth-century wit-masters in the creation of the image; to emphasize biographical facts which contributed a peculiar susceptibility to public acclaim; and to evaluate Holmes as a spokesman for the liberation of human beings from traditional dogma by scientific recognition of physical and mental cripplings. The medical scholar who brings professional studies to throw light on human relations is welcome today. Of such doctors, Holmes was one of the most penetrating and original, and he remains one of the sanest. The pictures he drew with vivid accuracy of New England village life have preserved a part of our American culture. The lively discussions of lasting human problems remain relevant; they are stimulating because of Holmes's probing intellect, his wide and perceptive experience of human behavior, and his apt phrasing.

In the early years of the twentieth century Dr. Oliver Wendell Holmes suffered the customary deflation of a personal and critical reputation which had been increasingly inflated during the preceding fifty years. The medical profession has continued to hold him in high esteem for his original diagnosis of puerperal fever as contagious and his challenge to doctors to stop destroying the new mothers under their care. A few poems had become an integral part of American culture, but his faith in human progress and in Christian charity was contrasted unfavorably with the timely skepticism and brilliant legal activities of his eldest son and namesake, Justice Oliver Wendell Holmes of the United States Supreme Court.

Three decades after the Justice's death the scales are tipping back. A new audience has been educated for the doctor's medical novels. The human wit and wisdom of the Autocrat still glow untarnished by the years. The moral sentiments are usually rendered palatable by the far-ranging, vivid figures expressing them. The danger today is that random memories attached to the name Oliver Wendell Holmes will fuse doctor and judge into one Yankee from Olympus who called Hemingway's stories garbage but who himself wrote a novel about a girl and a snake.

In this study of Dr. Holmes I have kept primarily to a chronological account because autobiographical echoes are so frequent in Holmes's prose and poetry that any other order would mean repetition. The more letters of Holmes that I have transcribed, the more I have become aware of the public image of him which was kept witty, apt, and gay no matter what was giving annoyance or worry in actual life. Therefore I have traced the evolution of the public image in his works in relation to events in his professional career or family life. I have anticipated chronologically only to treat the works in the Breakfast-Table series and the novels together, and to trace his career as poet for Harvard occasions. By viewing these three groups together, a comparative evaluation could be achieved. Even with my conscious attempt to follow a straight line in thus linking Holmes and Harvard, aspects of that relation tend to turn up at any moment, as they actually did in Holmes's life.

A mellow picture of the Boston essayist and poet in his professional and social relations was drawn by Mark Anthony DeWolfe Howe, Sr., in 1939. A soundly documented study of Holmes's career in medicine and authorship by Eleanor M. Tilton appeared in 1947. A definitive bibliography of Holmes was begun by the late Franklin T. Currier and completed by Eleanor M. Tilton in 1953. In order not to duplicate any of these recent works, I have emphasized chronology and completeness.

I have also stressed the ways Holmes was at odds with his own age with the object of correcting the impression that he merely voiced quickly and humorously the taste of his audiences, and "lived a life so uneventful that the utter absence of anything in it to remark upon became in itself remarkable." So wrote his wife's nephew, John Torrey Morse, in the official *Life and Letters* he brought out two years after Holmes's death. Apparently Morse was like Henry Adams and found *events* only in politics and Washington—natural perhaps for a man who was editor of the American Statesmen series and who wrote six of the biographies himself. But such an impression of Lethean tranquillity for a man who wrote and spoke or sang occasional poems for over fifty years, delivered lectures for forty, and confessed that "to write an anniversary poem . . . is itself a short fever" surely needs correction. Sometimes Holmes's creative experience was even more violent: "To write a lyric is like having a fit, you can't have one when you wish you could . . . and you can't help having it when it comes itself."

For the use of manuscripts, special printings, and documents of biographical or critical value, I am indebted to old friends of Dr. Holmes or to their descendants; to librarians, curators, private collectors; and to booksellers in many states and cities of the United States, in London, Birmingham, and Paris. The Library of Harvard University is rich in Holmes manuscripts, books, and association items, and I owe much to the generous help of Carolyn Jakeman in Houghton Library and of Clifford K. Shipton, Custodian of the Harvard University Archives. To successive directors and staff members of the Massachusetts Historical Society and the Boston Medical Library I am deeply grateful for the easy access they have consistently granted me to valuable Holmes holdings. I shall always be grateful to Holmes's grandson, the late Edward Jackson Holmes, for freely opening to me during several summers the largely untouched stores of books and manuscripts in the house at 296 Beacon Street.

Houghton Mifflin Company has kindly given me permission to quote from *The Writings of Oliver Wendell Holmes*, Riverside edition; *The Complete Poetical Works of Oliver Wendell Holmes*, edited by Horace E. Scudder, Cambridge edition; *A Bibliography of Oliver Wendell Holmes*, compiled by George B. Ives; and *The Life and Letters of Oliver Wendell Holmes* by John Torrey Morse, Jr.

MIRIAM ROSSITER SMALL

Wells College
Aurora, New York

Contents

Chronology

1809   August 29, born Cambridge, Massachusetts, eldest child of the Reverend Abiel and Sarah Wendell Holmes.

1824-   Student at Phillips-Andover Academy.
1825

1825-   Student at Harvard College; Class Poet of 1829.
1829

1829-   Student at Dane Law School, Cambridge.
1830

1830-   Student at Tremont Medical School; lived at No. 2 Central
1833   Court, Boston. On September 16, 1830, "Old Ironsides" in Boston *Daily Advertiser;* on March 26, 1831, "The Last Leaf" in *The Amateur;* in *New-England Magazine* for November, 1831, and February, 1832, two numbers of *The Autocrat of the Breakfast-Table.*

1833-   Medical student in Paris and traveler in Europe.
1835

1836   M.D. granted at Harvard Medical School; first volume of *Poems* published.

1838   *Bolyston Prize Dissertations for the Years 1836 and 1837* (On Intermittent Fever in New England, Neuralgia, and Direct Exploration in Medical Practice).

1839-   Professor of Anatomy at Dartmouth Medical College,
1840   Hanover, New Hampshire.

1840   June 15, married Amelia Lee Jackson, and went to live at 8 Montgomery Place, Boston.

1841   March 8, eldest child, Oliver Wendell Holmes, Jr., born.

1841-   Lyceum Lecturer.
1857

1842   *Homœopathy and Its Kindred Delusions.*

1843   October 20, daughter Amelia Jackson born. *The Contagiousness of Puerperal Fever.*

1846   October 17, son Edward Jackson born. In November, suggested name *anaesthesia* for new drug to render patients insensible.

1847-
1882   Professor of Anatomy (and Physiology until 1870) at Harvard Medical School; Dean, 1847-53.

1849-
1856   Spent summers on old Wendell estate in Pittsfield, Massachusetts.

1851   Began writing annual Class Poem for meetings.

1857   October, became member of Saturday Club. Began *The Autocrat of the Breakfast-Table* in the first number of *Atlantic Monthly* (November); published as book in 1858.

1858   Moved to 21 Charles Street, Boston.

1859   *The Professor at the Breakfast-Table.*

1860-
1861   *Elsie Venner* (novel).

1861   April, son Oliver Wendell Holmes, Jr., enlisted in Union Army; wounded three times in succeeding years of fighting.

1862   "My Hunt After 'The Captain'" in December *Atlantic; Songs in Many Keys.*

1864   *Soundings from the Atlantic;* a collection of essays previously published.

1867   *The Guardian Angel* (novel).

1870   Moved into new house at 296 Beacon Street.

1871   "Dorothy Q.: A Family Portrait"; gambrel-roofed house in Cambridge sold to Harvard.

1872   *The Poet at the Breakfast-Table.*

1875   *Songs of Many Seasons.*

1878   Bought summer home at Beverly Farms; *John Lothrop Motley.*

1879   December 3, *Atlantic* "Breakfast" to celebrate Holmes's seventieth birthday (August 29).

1880   *The Iron Gate.* Awarded honorary degree of LL.D. by Harvard.

1882   Became Professor Emeritus of Harvard Medical School.

1883 *Medical Essays 1842-1882; Pages from an Old Volume of Life.*

1885 *Ralph Waldo Emerson; A Mortal Antipathy* (novel).

1886 April-August, traveled in England, Scotland, and France with daughter Amelia; awarded honorary degrees in June by Cambridge, Edinburgh, and Oxford universities.

1887 *Our Hundred Days in Europe.*

1888 *Before the Curfew.* Wife Amelia died in February.

1889 Daughter Amelia died in April. Oliver Wendell Holmes, Jr., and wife came to live at 296 Beacon Street. Harvard awarded Dr. Holmes the honorary A.M. he had requested.

1890 *Over the Teacups;* "The Broomstick Train."

1891 Riverside edition of *Writings* with new prefaces by Holmes.

1894 October 7, died at 296 Beacon Street. Funeral October 10, in King's Chapel.

Oliver Wendell Holmes

CHAPTER *1*

Family and Education

I *Honorable Ancestry*

IN HIS WRITINGS Oliver Wendell Holmes has much to say about the importance of an honorable ancestry. He has stressed the security that comes from long lines of ancestors in one place who have played a worthy part in cultural and political life. What he has not often mentioned, but what mattered to him as much as ancestry all his life long, was acceptance and popularity. The irresistible lure the speaker's platform came to have for him was the result of this susceptibility to public acclaim. Such a susceptibility was probably natural for a youth who was the eldest son of a minister caught between two sides of a theological quarrel so bitter that the father was ultimately dismissed from the most important church in Cambridge. The security of ancestry was present for the boy to experience too: the minister's family lived in a fine Wendell house, and the Wendell ancestry was a living part of the boy's existence. But the creation of a public image which was always secure and at ease probably would not have evolved so soon or lasted so long if the youth had not known security and insecurity side by side.

Born in Cambridge, Massachusetts, on August 29, 1809, Oliver Wendell Holmes was the third child and eldest son of the Reverend Abiel Holmes and his second wife, Sarah Wendell Holmes. Pastor of the First Church in Cambridge, Abiel Holmes held more strictly to orthodox beliefs and ways of worship and preaching than did many of his congregation. The more liberal ways of the Wendell family, their heritage and position, mattered more to the growing boy than did his father's orthodoxy. Judge Oliver Wendell, Sarah's father, had bought the gambrel-roofed house across from Cambridge Common for his daughter, and he lived there with her until his death in 1812. Another Wendell inheritance was the first summer home Holmes had after his own family was established, which was part of the old Wendell estate in Pittsfield, Massachusetts.

The first Wendell, Evert Jansen, had come from Emden, East Friesland [Holland] in 1640, and settled in Albany. In the early eighteenth century, Jacob Wendell came to Boston and by his marriage to Sarah Oliver gave Holmes two noted ancestresses. Anne Bradstreet, author of the first book of poems by an American writer (*The Tenth Muse Lately Sprung Up in the Americas* [London, 1650]), was the daughter of one governor of the Massachusetts Bay Colony, Thomas Dudley (1634-40; 1645-50); the wife of another, Simon Bradstreet (1679-86; 1689-92); and the grandmother of Mercy Bradstreet, who married Dr. James Oliver and had a daughter, Sarah Oliver, who was Holmes's great grandmother. Dorothy Quincy became famous through Holmes's poem "Dorothy Q." (1871), and his opening of "Grandmother's mother" is accurate. The son of Sarah Oliver and Jacob Wendell, the Honorable Oliver Wendell, married Mary Jackson, daughter of Edward Jackson and Dorothy Quincy (b. 1709); and their daughter Sarah was Holmes's mother. A foreword to the poem, which is subtitled "A Family Portrait," cites Dorothy's relative Edmund and the two Josiahs as indicative of Quincy prestige[1]

Although his Holmes ancestors never came so close to Wendell* as did the Wendells, Jacksons, and Quincys, he did go in May and in June of 1866 to Woodstock, Connecticut, to supplement what he had found about the Holmes family in his father's notes and diaries, by visiting graveyards, sites, and old inhabitants. The most publicized visit Holmes made to Woodstock was in 1877 for the Fourth of July celebration at which he read "A Family Record" (239-42). Wealthy merchant-publisher Henry Chandler Bowen[2] and his sons made much of this annual festival in the park they had given the town, and the popular occasional poet who had paternal roots in Woodstock was a natural choice as guest of honor. Holmes was suffering so severely from asthma when he left Boston that he was reluctant to make visits, but he did prepare a poem to deliver in his father's native town. The poem mentioned several Holmes ances-

---

* The name *Wendell* was always used by family and friends to address both this Oliver Wendell Holmes and his son and namesake.

tors and closed with tender lines about the portrait of grandfather Dr. David and his own father:

> . . . Nay, surely there I trace
> The hinted outlines of a well-known face!
> Not those the lips for laughter to beguile,
> Yet round their corners lurks an embryo smile,
> The same on other lips my childhood knew
> That scarce the Sabbath's mastery could subdue.

He closed with loving memories of "The Scholar Son . . . whose
breathing form was once so dear, / Whose cheering voice was
music in my ear." Although the poem was the proper occasional
one he had learned to execute with unfailing success, the tone
and reference suggest something deeper than perfunctory remark.

The first Holmes to come to this country was John, who arrived
in 1686. He came directly to Woodstock, Connecticut, where he
was surveyor and substantial citizen who gave the common in
South Woodstock for public use. His son David was known
only as Deacon, but the second David was Holmes's grandfather,
a captain in the French and Indian Wars and a surgeon during
the Revolution. He married Temperance Bishop of Norwich,
Connecticut, and Abiel Holmes was born December 24, 1763.
Although Captain-Doctor David died in 1779, Temperance
Holmes managed the estate so capably and so independently—she
refused to remarry—that Abiel went to Yale College and was
never restricted in his serious desires. He graduated from Yale
in 1783, with honors and a respectable part at commencement,
and continued at the college as tutor and student of theology;
his ties with Woodstock remained close until his mother's death
in August, 1803.

On November 1, 1790, Abiel Holmes married Mary Stiles,
daughter of Ezra Stiles, president of Yale, with whom he had
studied theology and from whom he gained a thorough grounding
in orthodox Calvinism. His first pastorate was in the Congrega-
tional Church in Midway, Georgia, but he and his wife remained
there only a year because of ill-health brought on by the
Southern climate. On January 25, 1792, he was installed as
pastor of the First Church in Cambridge, and immediately
Harvard honored him with an A.M. degree. After his first wife
died on August 29, 1792, the handsome, cultivated widower
was considered eminently eligible by the young ladies of

Cambridge; one of them wrote an acquaintance: "I am going to surprise you. Mr. Abiel Holmes, of Cambridge, whom we so kindly chalked out for Miss N. W. is going to be married, and, of all folks in the world, guess who to. Miss Sally Wendell. I am sure you will not believe it; however, it is an absolute fact, for Harriot and M. Jackson told Miss P. Russell, who told us; it has been kept secret for six weeks, nobody knows for what."[3] The marriage took place on March 26, 1801; the surprise about the thirty-eight-year-old minister's choice may have derived from his wife's age—she was only five years younger than he—or because she had not joined the chase.

The first offspring of the marriage was Mary Jackson (January 17, 1802—June 14, 1825), who was named for Mrs. Holmes's mother and was so eager a reader that she won the ancient Dutch Bible inherited from the first Wendell in this country—it was to go to the child who could read passages from the Bible correctly at the earliest age. In 1822, she chose from among her many suitors Dr. Usher Parsons of Providence, and died in 1825, at the birth of her son Charles Parsons. This lad, who had a second home with his Cambridge relatives, followed his father and Uncle Wendell in the study of medicine. Ann Susan, born in 1804, the second child, was ready to become *Miss Holmes* in 1822, when her sister Mary went to Providence to live. Although brother Wendell sorely missed the bright face and merry ways of Mary, he enjoyed telling her of Ann's other suitors[4] besides the favored Charles Wentworth Upham[5] of Salem whom she married on March 29, 1826. Like her brother Wendell she cherished the maternal heritage: one son was named Oliver Wendell and one daughter Dorothy Quincy. The third daughter, Sarah Lathrop, was born December 29, 1805, and died November 6, 1812.

The literary offspring of the Reverend Abiel Holmes in 1805, his two-volume *American Annals,* lived longer; a second edition appeared in 1826, and it still has a place in American history as the first attempt to record events on this side of the Atlantic as *American* rather than *Colonial.* This careful scholarly work was responsible for his being made a Fellow of the American Academy of Arts and Sciences and a member of both the Massachusetts Historical Society and the American Philosophical Society. He deserved the "admirable annalist" he was called,[6] even if his elder son noted that his historical writings were "eminent, more for patience and accuracy than for metaphysical subtlety or extended range."[7]

The advent of his son, the minister noted precisely in his almanac for 1809, opposite the date August 29: "Son b."; on September 10, the baptism of Oliver Wendell Holmes was entered by his father in the parish register. He was named for his mother's father, "the aged owner," whom he just remembered —he died when Wendell was three—in one of the "rooms of the second story, the chambers of birth and death, . . . sacred to silent memories."[8] The deaths were those of Judge Oliver Wendell and of Sarah Lathrop in 1812; and early in that year was a birth—the last child. He, John Holmes, was graduated from Harvard in 1832, and he received a law degree at the Harvard Law School in 1836. Always remaining a bachelor with the memory of a fiancée who early died of consumption, John devoted himself to his mother and lived with her in the old house in Cambridge until after her death on August 19, 1862. When the house was finally sold to Harvard in April, 1871, he moved to rooms in the house of his former housekeeper, and he lived at No. 5 Appian Way until his death in 1899. Plagued by a knee injury and later by eye trouble, he was the cherished companion of a few close friends, among them James Russell Lowell. He took little part in any external activity save for three trips abroad—in 1839, 1872, and 1882.[9]

In an essay about the old house in Cambridge, which Holmes admitted he was writing partly because of the warm response to his poem "Dorothy Q.," he wrote of the happy days of his childhood there. It had a cellar and an attic for exploration and for ghosts; its clerical visitors were sometimes cheerful and welcome, sometimes melancholy, cheerless, and dreaded. Holmes expressed doubts that the dents in the floor of the study had been made by the musket butts of the Continental militia the night before the battle of Bunker Hill, but he had no doubt that Warren slept there that night. The Revolution was near in those days: his mother could remember being hurried as a child of six from Boston to Newburyport to escape the British soldiers.

The garret, "'a realm of darkness and thick dust, and shroudlike cobwebs," contained besides the cradle, chair, and bed of his Grandfather Wendell, "the large wooden reel which the bleareyed deacon sent the minister's lady, who thanked him graciously, and twirled it smilingly, and in fitting season bowed it out ecently to the limbo of troublesome conveniences" (III, 24). This gracious warm-hearted action, together with the practical solution, was typical of all reports of Sarah Wendell. From a background of liberal belief, comfortable living, taste, and culture, she brought to her children a quick understanding which attained for them a piano and dancing-lessons. She also made it easy for her husband to relax, with the majority of the members of his church, from the harsh orthodoxy of the Calvinistic doctrine and worship which he had known in Connecticut, especially at Ezra Stiles's college in New Haven.

II *Childhood, Education*

Instead of fighting battles with the Devil for the possession of his own soul, as a child brought up in the shadow of eternal damnation very well might, young Wendell's battles were fought on "his arid patch of earth" against "the professional specialist in the shape of grub, caterpillar, aphis, or other expert" which were lurking to "murder the whole attempt at vegetation" (III, 21). Both parents approved his battles in the garden, but they gave him a sound scolding when he took five-year-old brother John to witness the last hanging in Gallows Lot on Jones's Hill in 1817.

His love of books began early, and he traced it to his early surroundings more than once: "It is a good thing to have some of the blood of these old ministers in one's veins"; it could be thanked "for a probable inheritance of good instincts, a good name, and a bringing up in a library where he bumped about among books from the time when he was hardly taller than one of his father's or grandfather's folios " (VIII, 410-11). A volume of poems impressed him especially because some pages were torn out with his father's note "Hiatus haud deflendus [an omission by no means to be regretted]." The poems were Dryden's, and on one page lines about *Bears* were crossed out because, the boy thought, they were too frightening for children; the man understood that Dryden's Protestant *Bears* in *The Hind and the Panther* would have to be blotted out with doctrinal horror by any devout Calvinist. In the "Library Hospital" which young Wendell often visited in the attic, he made many strange acquaintances, among them *The Negro Plot.* Doubtless sent to

Abiel Holmes by a Southern friend, it told of the dreaded insurrection of the Negroes; it helped to keep the son from being a convert to the abolitionist activities of William Lloyd Garrison.

The first handwriting of Oliver Wendell Holmes which has been preserved reveals that his cheerful confidence about the reward of good works began at the age of five. Framed and hanging on the wall in his last home at 296 Beacon Street, and kept there as long as the house remained the home of his grandson, are very early records of his wife Amelia Jackson and himself. At the top is a printed form, with her name and the date written in: "Affectionate approbation is bestowed upon Amelia Jackson January 1 1822." Below is a water-color drawing of a brown horse on a green background; on the back is drawn a heart within which is written in ink: "Good boys generally meet with a reward for their good behaviour and certainly so will · O W H." Below Abiel Holmes had dated it *"May 1814."* The affectionate approbation Amelia Jackson had won at the age of four she continued to win throughout her life. These were probably mementoes from the dame schools they attended. Young Wendell went to Dame Prentiss' whence he may have proudly borne home his drawing and the motto; his brightening a moral statement by making it personal was an innate habit of thought rather than an acquired rhetorical flourish. Fortunately Abiel Holmes was a careful historian who set down dates.

Young Wendell's next school was Master William ("Sawney") Biglow's; Biglow cared more for wit and verse-writing than for drilling and figures, and the lad was a favorite pupil. From 1819 to 1824, he attended the "Port School," private and recently established in Cambridgeport for children of the college community in Cambridge and of the business community in Cambridgeport. Holmes later admitted to jealousy of the superiority of schoolmate Margaret Fuller, whose talk was "affluent, magisterial, *de haut en bas*"; he gratefully acknowledged, however, the leadership of Richard Henry Dana in organizing the "Cambridge-chucks" against the "Port-chucks"; and he enjoyed his share in the battles, though his efforts were more in quick, effective words than in blows since, though wiry and agile, he was small for his years (VIII, 240-43). His first surviving poem dates from this period; again it was apparently preserved by his father, with a date and a note:

Theme given to OWH. detained at home 24 July 1822

"Perdidi diem." Tiberias.

"I've lost a day," old Tibby said,
Then sighed and groaned, and went to bed.
This monarch, as they said of old,
Knew time was worth much more than gold.
I'm of this sage opinion too,
And think this man judged pretty true.
But now, my friends, I'll bid good bye,
Now you are tired—and so am I.

———————

Exact *copy* of what he wrote in a short time with his pencil and delivered to his father.

A.H.

Not very bright for a boy nearly 13 years old in my private opinion. OWH. June 27th 1871[10]

The rhyming couplet used by the boy was the poetic form he would naturally turn to: his father had employed the heroic couplet in his poetic attempts, as was to be expected from a scholar familar with Dryden, Pope, and the many didactic verse-writers of the seventeenth and eighteenth centuries. Abiel Holmes probably had no more use for Samuel Butler's burlesque of the Puritans in *Hudibras* than he had for Dryden's *Bears*, but he was scholar enough to know that *Hudibras* had established the octosyllabic couplet as the proper form for familiar verse, and to appreciate his small son's easy and appropriate use of the form.

The facility young Wendell exhibited in this "Theme" marked a variety of his accomplishments: they ranged from whittling and whispering to smoking cigars and playing the flute. To help him focus his quick response and develop concentration, he was sent in 1824-25 to study at Phillips Academy in Andover before he entered Harvard College. No doubt his father was glad to have him settled for a year in that center of Calvinistic orthodoxy, where the theological school influenced both academy and town. The son who, as late as 1871, wrote Harriet Beecher Stowe that he "even to that day didn't read novels on Sunday, at least until 'after sundown,'" admitted it was not from duty or religion so much "as a tribute to the holy superstitions of more innocent years, before I began to ask my dear good father those *enfant terrible* questions which were so much harder to answer than anything he found in St. Cyrian and Tarretin and the other old books I knew the smell of so well, and can see now, standing in their old places" (Morse, II, 230).

A homesick lad was left in August, 1824, at the home of Dr. James Murdock, a professor at the Theological Seminary, by his father and mother, who had driven him the twenty miles from Cambridge. "Sea-sickness and home-sickness are hard to deal with by any remedy save time," he wrote twenty-five years later. But the year in Andover proved rich in new experiences and friends which, along with the arguments, exhibitions, and rambles, he later remembered more than the lectures, sermons, or doctrinal impact of the school. Young Wendell's accent on the material things of the world about him suggests a real link with writers of the eighteenth century, but the emphasis was as much innate as the result of early reading. In 1893, he noted that he had first seen in Andover "red looking vegetables in the garden which I took for red peppers, but found to be what were called 'love-apples' or *tomatoes*." Persis, "whose humble, but useful services were so important to all of us," was well-meaning but the "blue and white soda-powder" she mingled with water and gave him to drink proved a mocking *fiz* for home-sickness and "struck a colder chill to my despondent heart" (VIII, 245). Another medical detail from Andover days was still present in his mind in his last year: when Dr. Murdock was ill to delirium, he uttered a prescription for himself in Latin: "emp sinapis pone collum [buy mustard, put on neck]."[11]

In those days of severe punishments in schools, this lad escaped with surprisingly few, if we take his word that he was "an inveterate whisperer," that he read other than schoolbooks during school-hours, and that his alert eye and mind were often caught by the extracurricular. That the ferule was applied to his palm in the Port School he recalls; but the cruel feruling took place at Andover when Jonathan Clement lost his temper and turned the boy's hand black with beating. The cause has not been noted in the many references to it by Holmes and others, but the sympathy was all with the lad: more than twenty years later Clement called on his former pupil to unburden his conscience with a personal apology (Morse, I, 24). Holmes's best friend was Phineas Barnes, "a fine rosy-faced boy" from Portland, Maine, with whom he formed a lasting friendship kept up by letters when Barnes went to Bowdoin and Holmes to Harvard and later during the years of rare meetings.

The most memorable debate for Holmes was a public one between himself and Barnes on Mary Queen of Scots. Later he noted his argument had been developed rhetorically and sentimentally as opposed to Barnes's closer and more logical treatment; the result was that "My sentences were praised and his conclusions adopted" (VIII, 250). A verse translation he made from Virgil was delivered and preserved (321); the mature Holmes found fault with his cockney rhyme of *arm* and *calm*. His highest distinction at Andover was won by his poem "Fancy," which he wrote and delivered at the great final Exhibition. Later he deprecated the youthful exuberance of figure and diction, but its success with its audience, young and old alike, encouraged him in the constant writing of verse. How happily he turned to verse is illustrated by lines preserved by the maid in the Cambridge home. One hot day in the summer of 1825, he was sitting in the shade on the lawn when a tramp asked for food. He took a piece of the newspaper he was reading, penned the following lines, and sent them by the tramp to the maid in the kitchen:

> Charitable Ann—
> Give this poor man—
> As much as you can—
> A little meat
> And bread to eat
> And a shady seat—
>
> —————
>
> O. W. Holmes.[12]

The evidence these lines give of the youth's natural bent for rhyme has some significance; but more significant is the ease he reveals in the use of triple rhyme and short lines before he became acquainted with French and Italian verse forms. Another characteristic feature of his writing made an early appearance: his sisters were often struck by the vividness or surprise of his comparisons, as when he compared the fair skin of a lovely girl to slack lime (Morse, I, 47).

III *College and Poetry*

From 1825 to 1830 Holmes was studying in Cambridge as a member of the Class of 1829 at Harvard College and at the Dane Law School. During his first three years at college he lived at home, but he was by no means shut off from active participation in the social life of the college. He belonged to clubs, well known and long-lived like the "Hasty Pudding," or short-lived and private like the "Puff" and the "Medical Faculty." The "Puff" was primarily for smoking "segars," but wine and talk also contributed and were more often present than "the Goddesss of Wisdom" (Morse, I, 50). The "Medical Faculty" was elaborately set up as a burlesque of examining candidates and of awarding or withholding degrees. Public figures were chosen as candidates, and those on the campus, like the stout and dogmatic Professor Popkin of classics, sometimes brought the fire nearer home. This club issued a catalogue which was a parody of the Harvard Triennial Catalogue, the aim being "to produce amusement by its mock solemnity, and the contrast between its pompous titles and its real nature" (letter of Holmes to Barnes of January, 1829; Morse, I [52]).

Holmes confessed to not being a devoted student, but he got high enough marks to be elected to Phi Beta Kappa in his senior year. The old curriculum offered him Rhetoric under Edward Tyrrel Channing, where exercises in speaking and writing gave him valuable training as a future lecturer and public speaker, and helped confine his "turgid rhetoric." His keenest intellectual response was to chemistry in his junior year, to mineralogy in his senior. His class petitioned for and was granted permission to choose a course in science instead of further study in Greek. He took advantage of the courses in modern foreign languages Ticknor was offering; he did well in French and Italian, less well in Spanish.

Holmes continued to write verses, probably most often for private social meetings. For public occasions the youth had already learned that, because of his five-feet-three height, blue eyes, and nondescript hair, he had to rely on wit and alertness rather than personal appearance to make an impression. He took part in Exhibitions during his junior and senior years: in the autumn of 1827, he read a verse translation of Catullus; on April 28, 1829, he read an original poem, "Forgotten Ages," a perfunctory account of poets and poetry, conventional in form and content. As Class Poet he wrote and delivered on July 14, 1829, a poem he made humorously familiar by the brief account of his "hapless amour with too tall a maid" and by invoking the ladies present as not too ideal "goddesses." His part at commencement on August 26, consisted of another original poem, in which the ladies present were addressed as "Fair creatures kindling with a starlike glow / The Hallowed precincts of the lofty row." Flattery was duly mingled with satire and an audience wearied by two hours of serious speeches applauded vigorously and gave him the praise for which he was already listening. More surprising than his writing verses was his belonging to the academic militia, "the Harvard Washington corps," which "parades before the ladies in the afternoon, and there is eating and drinking and smoking and making merry" (letter of Holmes to Barnes of October, 1828; Morse, I, 59). The students enjoyed festivities after the Exhibitions: for Holmes's appearance in April, 1829, his room in Stoughton Hall was so stocked with wine that conviviality lasted beyond the night of the important day.

One reason that Holmes lived on campus during his senior year and that his parents contributed wine so generously to make Exhibition Day festive for him and his friends was the strain and distress in the old gambrel-roofed house across the Common. Today we know of the revolt of Channing and the Unitarians, of Emerson, Thoreau, and the Transcendentalists, and we conclude there was a general relaxation of the stern tenets of Calvinism by the 1830's. On the contrary, supporters of orthodox belief and practice were many and so influential that well past the middle of the nineteenth century they were investigating and arbitrarily dismissing too liberal ministers and professors. The fight was joined with the fierceness of a rearguard action, and Cambridge was a natural battleground, with the dangerous liberal and Unitarian tendencies emanating from college faculty and students. The Reverend Abiel Holmes never turned his back on the orthodox principles in which he had been trained; but, less a theologian than a scholar, he accepted the broadening ways about him in Cambridge naturally and easily; he exchanged pulpits freely with neighboring ministers without inquiring into their doctrine.

The *Boston Recorder*, an orthodox paper often made eloquently denunciatory by Lyman Beecher, was on the lookout for back-sliders, and it reminded the Reverend Abiel Holmes he should be more strictly doctrinal. By July, 1827, as a result of his stricter observances, his parish had prepared a memorial and presented it to him. This memorial, from the more liberal group which was in the majority in the parish, did not ask him to change his doctrine: it requested he resume free exchange and continue his less doctrinally severe sermons. The orthodox party in the church was fewer in number than the liberal but louder and more contentious; the gentle scholar who was "thoroughly imbued with the doctrines of Calvinism, modified by the kindly nature in which they were received" (Morse, I, 37), was caught between the two warring camps. Councils and committees met and debated, and on May 19, 1829, the parish dismissed its pastor; on June 7, 1829, the Reverend Abiel Holmes preached his last sermon in the parish church. The orthodox party moved to the courthouse, and he continued preaching there; but the next year a strictly orthodox assistant pastor was brought in and the elder Holmes's position became more humiliating and unhappy as he was forced into a narrow belligerence he did not enjoy.[13] Until his death in 1837, the one sign of late recognition Abiel Holmes received was for the scholar; in 1832, Allegheny College in Meadville, Pennsylvania awarded him the honorary degree of Doctor of Laws.

His father's doctrinal stand and unhappiness when his ortho-doxy made him rejected by his parish and also unsatisfactory to the rigid authoritarians permanently affected Oliver Wendell Holmes. His early disagreement with his father's doctrine is reflected in the questions of the *enfant terrible*, as he called himself. "When it came to the threats of future punishment as described in the sermons of the more hardened theologians, my instincts were shocked and disgusted beyond endurance." His autobiographical notes contain his often-quoted: "No child can overcome these early impressions without doing violence to the whole mental and moral machinery of his being. He may conquer them in after years, but the wrenches and strains which his victory has cost him leave him a cripple as compared with a child trained in sound and reasonable beliefs" (Morse, I, 39-40). The evidence of human reason and later of medical and psychological research he constantly opposed to theological dogma, and his rational, liberal belief concerned itself with promoting human healing and happiness and not with delivering judgment and punishment. At the slightest hint, he started down the path that explained human weaknesses by psychological and physical influences that not only made personal responsibility absurd but also rendered unacceptable the strict logic of human sin and punishment as expounded by Jonathan Edwards. Because he did express his own convictions so frequently, so eloquently, and so acceptably to an American society gradually relaxing from strict theological dogma into humanitarian emphases, no trace of mental or moral crippling may be found in the son; in his note he may well be reflecting "wrenches and strains" he saw his father suffering. But the son's preoccupation with the harsh slavery that dogma could cause as well as the high value he gave to popularity and social acceptance are owing to these youthful years of uneasiness of family position and of partial rejection in Cambridge.

Another incident stirred him against the orthodox church party in these years: in January, 1828, Dr. James Murdock, at whose home he had lived in Andover, was in trouble at Andover Theological Seminary for some lapse of doctrine and was dismissed. Sixty-five years later Holmes was still distressed by this, when he noted in a letter to Murdock's daughter of June 10, 1893, that her father was too learned and too honest "to suit those old cast-iron Calvinists." Holmes rejoiced that Murdock "got free from them at last and had full scope for his fine scholarship in the work he best loved"—as Abiel Holmes had not. That the son was still sensitively aware of theological attitudes was evident in his comment that Murdock was "too enlightened for the custodians of that iron-bound Seminary which of late has been bursting its hoops and spilling its orthodoxy."

The controversial situation of the Holmes family in the Cambridge parish contributed as much as his dislike of his law studies and the unavailability of feminine companions to his confiding to Barnes in January, 1830, "I am sick at heart of this place and almost everything connected with it" (Morse, I, 65). But the only expression of personal reaction to the controversy was written later to his father's friend, the Reverend William Jenks, who had addressed to the family questions in connection with his proposed biography of the deceased Reverend Abiel Holmes. After Wendell had consulted with his mother and brother and they had decided against making public the minister's private journals or giving specific information about the situation he had faced in Cambridge, Wendell wrote:

—Nor is there much in his theological career upon which I can dwell with pleasure. For many years quietly established at Cambridge, he was respectably but not conspicuously stationed as a minister—. There was hitherto little in his long career to attract notice to his pulpit. He maintained a kind of middle station between the opposing parties, as yet unmolested. The time having come when he stood in the way of the theological tacticians then managing the church militant, he was sacrificed.— His course as a clergyman, peculiarly delicate and difficult, amidst the conflicting opinions which raged round him showed all the amiability and some of the weaknesses of his character.— But his last years were tranquil, and we may try to forget those scenes in which, alas, he suffered for himself while he acted for others.

.   .   .   .

In our opinion it is in his historical capacity chiefly that my father's life should be treated. His religious life, in any considerable detail, cannot be wanted by the more liberal sects of our vicinity and our city, for his principles of faith were the old orthodox party—nor by the present orthodox party—for it was by their agency that he was torn in his old age from his people, and finally rejected and supplanted in his authority . . . the two great parties which divide our community crowded against him each from its own side—one pressing upon his Calvinistic faith, the other upon his liberal principles of intercourse and orderly habits of public ministration, with much care and policy for their own interests, and too little anxiety with regard to him . . . God forbid that at this period the machinery of modern Jesuitism should be unfolded as it was brought to bear upon my father's happiness.[14]

This succinct summary of the conflict involving his father and the family's position in Cambridge was drawn from Holmes because the request of a respected friend could not be ignored; and it was written after a respite of two years of study abroad had done little to soften his hurt and anger. The single personal statement forced from him reveals why his scorn for orthodoxy and its methods was emotionally intense as well as supported rationally by all the evidence he was constantly gathering from medical studies and social observations; it also explains why that scorn and his unending attacks on dogma carried no personal bitterness against his father.

The year after college, 1829-30, Holmes was living at home while studying at the Dane Law School that had recently been strengthened by the presence of Judge Joseph Story and J. H. Ashmun and by many more students. It was an important year for Holmes the poet. *The Collegian* was started by John O. and Epes Sargent, still students at Harvard, and it ran for six numbers (February-July, 1830). Like Addison and Steele's *Spectator* papers and Irving's Salmagundi Club papers in New York a few years earlier, fictitious names of the club members were signed to various articles. Holmes was merely a contributor, and his poems were unsigned; but of the twenty-five pieces he contributed, four were accepted in the canon of his verse: "The Dorchester Giant" (10-11), "Reflections of a Proud Pedestrian" (8-9), "Evening / By a Tailor" (9-10), and "The Height of the Ridiculous" (14). The closing lines of the last poem may be taken as a kind of perennial resolution the young author formed: "And since, I never dare to write / As funny as I can." Five more of these early printings were added as some of the "Verses from the Oldest Portfolio" in the Riverside edition of his poems (XIII, 235-78); six, in the posthumous Cambridge edition (321-25).

The first group of Holmes's poems to be collected appeared, unsigned and with poems by others, in a pamphlet in Boston in 1830: *Illustrations of the Athenaeum Gallery of Paintings.* For four years the Boston Athenaeum had been holding an annual exhibit of paintings which supplemented its permanent collections, and this catalogue for 1830 offered a "liquid flow of song" instead of the usual description and criticism. The nine poems by Holmes in this publication had all appeared previously in Frederic S. Hill's weekly *New-England Galaxy* or in his semimonthly *Amateur.* Only one of the nine poems has been remembered: "The September Gale," which celebrated the hurricane of September 23, 1815, is genuinely humorous and familiar as he rhymes his Sunday *breeches* with *witches* and *stitches* (13-14).

Another poem from 1830 has emerged from the Appendix to which it was relegated in the Riverside and Cambridge editions, to appear in a modern College Anthology of American Literature—"The Ballad of the Oysterman." First printed in the *Amateur* of July, 1830, it began a long history as a song on the stage of the Chatham Theatre in New York on March 15, 1831, with the title "Love and Oysters. Parody on Hero and Leander. . . ." For that performance the singer and the air were named, but not the author. Through the century to 1894, the verses were set to music by three different composers, sometimes with minor changes to suit the music or singer; with each, Holmes was named as author. This popularity stemmed partly from the easy singing meter, seven-beat couplet lines arranged as quatrains; partly from the incongruous detail used for mythical lovers: ". . . he was taken with the cramp"; "And now they keep an oyster-shop for mermaids down below" (322-30).

The poem Holmes wrote in 1830, which brought him national attention immediately and has continued to be linked with his name, was "Old Ironsides." On September 14, 1830, the Boston *Daily Advertiser* carried a note copied from the New York *Journal of Commerce* of September 10, a note often reprinted with the poem "Old Ironsides" (3-4). The article deprecated the announced plan of the United States Navy to scrap the frigate *Constitution*, historically the most renowned vessel of the nation; it contrasted such action unfavorably with England's just and honorable preservation of Nelson's flagship *Victory* which he had commanded at the battle of Trafalgar. The youth was stirred to write three stanzas of eight lines each which saved the *Constitution* then, and, being revived and circulated as recently as 1944, have continued to save her. The rapid, ringing lines beginning "Ay, tear her tattered ensign down!" make us hear "the battle shout" and "the victor's tread"; the figure "The harpies of the shore shall pluck / The eagle of the sea!" prepares for the heroic close: "And give her to the god of storms, / The lightning and the gale!" The poem was first printed in the *Advertiser* on September 16. Introductory lines were added when it was made a part of the longer poem "Poetry" in the first edition of Holmes's poems (1836):

> And one, who listened to the tale of shame,
> Whose heart still answered to that sacred name,
> Whose eye still followed o'er his country's tides
> Thy glorious flag, our brave Old Ironsides!
> From yon lone attic, on a summer's morn,
> Thus mocked the spoilers with his school-boy scorn.

These personal lines about the poem's writing are convincingly easy and natural, but the youth they depict is only the public figure that Holmes wanted to present. Like the writers he knew so well from the early eighteenth century, he took an artistic pride in forming for his public the image he wanted seen; and he made this image convincing by the easy rhythm of his expression. There is nothing really revealing of the author in his early exercises in verse despite the frequent personal tone: they do not reflect his boredom with his law studies, his embarrassment over the theological quarrel which made the Holmes family unhappy in Cambridge, or his wanting "a girl in the neighborhood whose blood ever rose above the freezing point," or "even a cherry-cheeked kitchen girl to romance with occasionally" (Morse, I, 65).

IV *Medical Student, Europe*

In October, 1830, Holmes left Cambridge to begin the study of medicine under a group of five doctors connected with the Massachusetts Medical College (later the Harvard Medical School); he moved to a room in the boarding-house of Mrs. Brown at No. 2 Central Court, Boston, to attend medical lectures and to spend long hours at Massachusetts General Hospital, where he learned by following doctors through the wards and into the dissecting-rooms. By March, 1831, he had found a young lady from Maine who seemed to be as attracted to him as he was to her; but by February, 1832, she had returned to Maine and he did not follow her. Although he was tired of being dependent on his family for support, he was eager to go to Europe to study medicine. A possible career as poet and literary man received no serious consideration, although interest continued to be shown in his verses. Some of his earlier poems had been reprinted in gift-books; seventeen, all reprints, appeared in May, 1833, in *The Harbinger,* a book compiled to be sold in Faneuil Hall, Boston, at the fair put on by ladies raising money to support Dr. Samuel G. Howe's recently established New England Institution for the Education of the Blind.

Most important of these reprints was the short poem which, with "Old Ironsides," has been justly reckoned as Holmes's claim to real poetic achievement. "The Last Leaf" was published in the *Amateur* of March 26, 1831, signed with the initials

"O.W.H." That Holmes recognized its success is indicated by its being placed second only to "Old Ironsides" in all editions of his poems collected during his lifetime. Like the latter, it was suggested by the life around him; in this poem the suggestion came from the grandfather of novelist Herman Melville, Major Thomas Melville, who was conspicuous on the streets of Boston by reason of his cocked hat, knee breeches, and silver-buckled shoes; he was rumored to have been one of the rebels at the Boston Tea-Party. This poem therefore fulfilled Holmes's definition of poetry as "the power of transfiguring the experiences and shows of life into an aspect which comes from the imagination and kindles that of others" (15). The short rhyming lines at the middle and end of the eight six-line stanzas were purposely adopted to free him from the imitators already troubling him. The rhythm of the amusing details that identified the odd old figure was combined with a metaphor which conveyed humane understanding of the pathos of the age-youth dilemma faced by the "last leaf upon the tree" (5). The praise Poe and Lincoln later gave this poem Holmes knew of and cherished: Poe, "who was not always over civil in speaking of New England poets," made a copy of it as "an excellently well conceived and well managed specimen of versification"; Lincoln's partner Herndon wrote in 1867: "I have heard Lincoln recite it, praise it, laud it, and swear by it; it took Mr. Lincoln's fancy in all moods, and fastened itself on him as never poem on man. This I know."[15]

"My Aunt," another poem reprinted in *The Harbinger* in 1833, was first printed in the *New-England Magazine* for November, 1831, signed "O.W.H." Like "The Last Leaf," "My Aunt" is a figure from the past comically incongruous to the present age: a descendant of Pamela, constantly guarded against the assaults of a "rabid youth." The note of sympathy is conveyed here by a similar figure: the unnecessarily protected girl has become "one sad, ungathered rose / On my ancestral tree" (8). The poems became fewer in late 1830 and in 1831, indicating that Holmes was no longer "writing poetry like a madman" and that his serious interest in his new medical studies was quieting "the incipient rhymester." Although sometimes he still yearned to have "the undisputed mastery of a petticoat," his desire for travel had changed from "the plan à la Goldsmith" which had been haunting him in Cambridge; but, even as he had dreamed, he had known he did not play the fiddle well enough, nor were his countrymen as indulgent as the French had been to Goldsmith, to make a poet's wanderings with his song and his violin practicable.

One more writing, this one in prose, grew out of his experiences in Boston from 1830 to 1833. In the *New-England Magazine* for November, 1831, and February, 1832, appeared the *Autocrat of the Breakfast-Table*—a far cry from his successor twenty-five years later. But the pattern of a talker who dominated an assortment of people and got more or less appropriate responses from them was created. These writings in verse and prose were unsigned, or signed only with initials, and there is no evidence that the youth considered a literary career desirable or practicable in spite of "the intoxicating pleasures of authorship." A New England emphasis on work—preferably on work that was useful to society—as the first requirement of the good life and of human happiness was in his blood and in his home: "being occupied is the next thing to being happy" appears in one phrase or another consistently through his writings.

For a young man so sensitive to the material world about him, medical studies had "painful and repulsive aspects," often owing to the medical ignorance of the time. The "block and tackle rigged from the ceiling" in the operating-room indicated the shocking terrors surgery involved before anaesthesia, but Holmes responded to the emphasis placed on close observation and accurate notes, and especially to the humane approach to the patient which he admired in his favorite teacher, Dr. James Jackson.[16] His medical studies bore out the *enfant terrible* questions he had asked his father when he had contrasted actual examples of compassion and understanding with the harsh dogma of absolute personal responsibility for sin and the resultant damnation of the orthodox Calvinists. In the distressing scenes of physical suffering, his mind was instantly responsive to the scientific method of studying every detail of evidence carefully rather than following a fixed rule of medication that might be more fatal than the disease.

In order to get more advanced training than he was receiving from the five physicians who were supplementing lectures at the Medical College by the study of human anatomy and of the progress of specific cases in the hospital, he was sure he must go to Paris to study. The American names important in medicine, such as Jackson and Warren in Boston and Pepper in Philadelphia, were sending their sons to Paris as the place the best medical training was then available. That Holmes's desire to study abroad before taking his medical degree was earnest and deserving of respect is indicated not only by his asking further help from his parents but also by their giving it. The Wendell properties were not rising in value to make up for the minister's diminished income, Ann Upham's children were coming fast, and John was studying law. But the money Wendell needed was promised him; and late in March, 1833, he set out for Providence, where he got advice, commissions, and letters of introduction from his brother-in-law Dr. Parsons, then went on to New York where he sailed on the new packet *Philadelphia* on the first of April. At the American Hotel in New York he had met several Boston friends who were also sailing, among them Robert William Hooper, whose journals of the voyage, of the stopover in England, and of medical studies in Paris give some livelier details than Holmes recorded for his relatives. The voyage took twenty-three days, and during a week's delay in England Holmes went to see Nelson's flagship *Victory* and also visited Salisbury Cathedral, Stonehenge, and the Isle of Wight.

When he and Hooper finally got to Paris on May 14, 1833, they were glad to find Bowditch, James Jackson, and Jonathan Mason Warren, sons of well-known Boston scientists, already established and ready to advise them. Holmes was soon settled in a room on the Left Bank near the hospitals and the *École de Médecine*. He joined the group that followed the great pathologist and teacher, Pierre Charles Alexandre Louis, through the wards of *La Pitié* from seven-thirty to ten or eleven in the morning, with sometimes a lecture of an hour and a half afterwards. Then the Americans had breakfast together, preferably at the *Café Procope*, the café of Voltaire, Rousseau, and Fontenelle.

Holmes was called on soon to make speeches for occasions, but he did devote himself happily to his studies in the "concentrated scientific atmosphere" of Paris. Visiting Americans like Emerson and his classmate Isaac Morse of New Orleans, required diversion and showing around, but aside from an occasional visit to the opera and the strange experience of watching a *Combat des Animaux* (where bulldogs fought each other, a wolf, a bear, a wild boar, a bull, and a jackass), Holmes's days followed a pattern of visiting hospitals, attending lectures, dissecting, and study—with private lessons in French added for weeks. Breakfast at eleven and dinner at five became the rule, and by the end of the summer he felt himself the complete Frenchman. He did not travel during that first summer, as did many of his more affluent countrymen; he remained in Paris, studying and absorbing the language and the atmosphere. He later regretted his too rare attendance at the theatre, which was the best school for the language. More than once he went to see and hear Mademoiselle Mars, who even at fifty-eight proved herself deserving of the title "the most celebrated living actress." From his new cosmopolitan point of view he admonished his parents against fearing the theatre as harmful; the only other such display in his letters home was the superior tone to his brother John on the wasting of precious time in idleness.[17]

Holmes's unpleasant experience with traditional authority in the Cambridge parish made him especially welcome the atmosphere of free inquiry he found in Paris; he frequently contrasted the respect for sound reason in Paris with "the patriarchal authority" which threatened intellectual growth at home. The three principles he especially valued were: "not to take authority when I can have facts; not to guess when I can know; not to think a man must take physic when he is sick" (Morse, I, 109). He had begun to unlearn "the habit of drugging for its own sake" under Dr. Jacob Bigelow in Boston. This and the indiscriminate bleeding of eighteenth-century medical practice were effectually discouraged by the hours spent with Louis. Holmes summed up what he had learned in Paris later: "The love of truth, the habit of passionless listening to the teaching of nature, the most careful and searching methods of observation" (IX, 436). The great surgeon Baron Dupuytren commented to students as they followed him through the wards of the *Hôtel Dieu,* and he strengthened the young student's conviction that "cases thoroughly recorded and mathematically analyzed" would lead to trustworthy results. The longer he stayed in Paris the more opportunities he became aware of: the lectures of the popular young Gabriel Andral planted seeds which would bear fruit later, as he stressed the relation of hereditary defects and physical abnormalities to mental disease.

In September, 1834, Holmes was accepted as a member of the Society of Medical Observation, which met every Saturday evening for discussion and reports. The organization was recognized as highly competitive, and Boston and Philadelphia students vied for first place. Membership in this society made Holmes more determined to distinguish himself in Paris and to return prepared to play a leading role in his profession.[18] In contrast to the eager happiness he found in his medical studies in Paris, young Wendell Holmes suffered misery from two sources connected with his family in Cambridge. He received no letters from home until October 14, 1833. From March to October was a long time to be in a foreign land and to receive no word from home. He finally discovered the way to get the letters his family had been faithfully writing him: the express agent had sent his letters to the bank that had his letter of credit; although he went there every week for funds, it wasn't until October 14 that he asked the right clerk for letters. The clerk opened a drawer and took out a great pile he had been carefully stowing away.

The other distress was money, and how long funds would be coming to make further study and travel possible. In May, 1834, he had gone with Hooper and J. M. Warren on the travels every American student took as part of his experience abroad: Strasbourg, Frankfurt, the boat-trip on the Rhine, Holland, and England. The medical museums and exhibits the young students sought out would not be as interesting to Holmes's family as they were to him, but he wrote home about some, especially after they reached London and Edinburgh. In London Dr. Parsons' letter to Clift opened doors for them that would otherwise have been tight shut. He did not tell his family that the group attended Derby Day at Epson Downs; a full account of that had to wait for his return to England in 1886 (X, 6), when he did not need to worry about parental approval of such use of the money which was disappearing with frightening rapidity as he traveled. Probably more than once in his youthful days in Cambridge his parents had shown express disapproval of Wendell's irresistible attraction to fast and showy horses.

Although exuberant superlatives described both Heidelberg and Edinburgh as the most beautiful cities he had ever seen, the weariness of too rapid sightseeing, the worry about dwindling funds, and the heaviness of English people and food in contrast to the gay variety of both in Paris made the return there on September 3, 1834, welcome to Holmes. The funds he had been pleading for had not yet arrived, and he had to continue to borrow from his Philadelphia friend Stewardson until late in the month. The political situation between France and the United States was tense because of the French debt, and in Cambridge rumors of war with France were as unsettling as was the fear that Paris might become fascinating to a young man for other reasons than opportunities for medical study. An accident to his brother John's knee and a growing weakness in his father's health loomed larger in Cambridge than matchless opportunities for further study and for purchasing instruments, skeletons, and books. Enough money was sent to enable Wendell to pay his debts and continue his studies through March of 1835. He did get the trip to Italy he kept wanting more and more, and money enough to purchase some of the engravings, books, and instruments he felt were necessary for the medical scholar; but he did not get a third year of study in Paris. What that experience had meant for him he gave most fully in a letter of April, 1834:

> I have lived comfortably, liberally if you please, but in the main not extravagantly.—I have employed my time with a diligence that leaves no regrets. My aim has been to qualify as my faculties would allow me, not for a mere scholar, for a follower of other men's opinions, for a dependent on their authority, but for the character of a man, who has seen and therefore knows, who has thought and has therefore arrived at his own conclusions.—I have lived among a great, a glorious people—I have thrown my thoughts into a new language—I have received the shock of new minds and new habits. I have drawn close the ties of social relations with the best formed minds I have been able to find from my own country. . . . I hope you do not think your money wasted.[19]

The last sentence is needed to evaluate the self-portrait justly. It is a young man's defense of himself to his supporting parents; yet all external evidence proves it fair as well as sincere. His unquestioned absorption in his work was due partly to its fitting his personal taste and opinion: conclusions were drawn by an independent mind studying actual observations rather than being based on arbitrary authority. The gravest threat to the growth of an original medical thinker lay in the importance he gave to social acceptance. His pride in being accepted by those he admired and respected most was unduly sensitive because of the uneasy days in Cambridge during and after his father's dismissal by his church. In later years he could laugh at himself for such susceptibility: "I was always patient with those who thought well of me." But for the erstwhile popular speaker and poet, about to return to friends who had the habit of turning to him for sprightly verse or timely comment, it posed a grave threat.

While in Paris, in the groove of a regular program, he found it easy to refuse to be again infected with "the lead-poisoning" of authorship. In the autumn of 1834, when his old editor John Sargent and Dr. Samuel Gridley Howe had bought the *New-England Magazine*, they wrote to ask him to contribute. His reply to them, and to his family, about such contributions, was a firm negative. To Sargent he was flowery: "the blossoms of my flaunting youth have fallen, and I am watching day and night over the cold, green, unripened fruit that must supply their places"; to his parents he was firm but still showed a poet's love of figures: "I have entirely relinquished the business of writing for journals and shall say No, though Minerva and Plutus come hand in hand to tear me, the Cincinnatus of Science, from the ploughtail she has bidden me to follow. How much I must learn—how hard I must work, before I have wrought this refractory ore into good tough, malleable, ductile, elastic iron—" (Morse, I, 146, 144).

Thus a young man determined to continue his serious work as medical student and thinker sailed for home from Le Havre on the packet *Utica* on November 1, 1835, and arrived in New York on December 14, after a tedious passage of forty-three days.

CHAPTER 2

Medicine or Poetry?

YOUNG Oliver Wendell Holmes's determination to devote his time to medicine instead of poetry was tested during his first year at home. His immediate task was to prepare the essay needed for his medical degree at Harvard: he chose the subject he had specialized in abroad—diseases of the heart. Called A *Dissertation on Acute Pericarditis* and dated January 12, 1836, it was accepted at Harvard but was not published until 1937, when it was brought out in Boston by the Welch Bibliophilic Society. In February, 1836, he passed his examinations and was voted the degree of doctor of medicine. On May 22, he was made a member of the Massachusetts Medical Society. The subject for the Bolyston Medical Prize had been announced earlier, "Direct Exploration" ("How far are the external means of exploring the condition of the internal organs, to be considered useful and important in medical practice?"). The essay which Holmes wrote won the prize. The use of the stethoscope was more widely accepted in Paris than in Boston, but it was not new, and the clear, vivid writing contributed as much as the content to his winning the prize. The essay was recommended for publication, along with two others on the question, as Volume VII of the *Library of Practical Medicine,* generously endowed by Dr. George C. Shattuck. Therefore, by October of 1836, Holmes had acquired his M.D. at Harvard and written two medical essays, one of which won him his degree; the other, a prize and publication. He had also hung out his shingle at his old boarding-house, No. 2 Central Court, Boston, and had been appointed a visiting physician at the Boston Dispensary, a charitable hospital where he had a chance to follow the program of diagnosis and recording of cases he had learned in Paris.

I *Poems*

Holmes had actively started out on a medical career. But poetry was not entirely neglected. In January, 1836, Park Benjamin and Charles Fenno Hoffman had continued the *New-England Magazine* as the *American Monthly Magazine,* and the issues from February through April contained four new, unsigned poems by Holmes. On May 11, 1836, he was writing his old rival for Class Poet, the Reverend James Freeman Clarke, of his pleasure that Clarke had recognized his being the writer of "La Grisette" (326), and had commended it. Holmes's sentences reveal a poet absorbed in his act of creation: "Like everything tolerable I ever wrote, it was conceived in exultation and brought forth with pain and labor. The time at which any new thought strikes me is my Sybilline moment, but the act of composition, so exciting and so easy to some people, is a wearing business, attended with a dull, disagreeable sensation about the forehead—only from time to time it is interrupted by the simultaneous descent of some group of words or some unexpected image, which produces a burst of the most insane enthusiasm and self-gratulation, during which I commit puerile excesses of language and action" (Morse, II, 269-70).

Since he had not written a stanza abroad, he feared he was "high and dry upon the sand" and several friends agreed he had "fallen off." The altering of some words in the magazine publication of "The Last Reader" (14) helped reenforce his determination to renounce poetry and devote himself to medicine. But he had accepted the literary distinction of being Phi Beta Kappa poet at Harvard that year, and his verses were entitled "Poetry." He also accepted the invitation to read this poem at the commencement exercises at Brown University. Since Harvard Phi Beta Kappa poems were traditionally published, Holmes succumbed to the temptation to collect his previously published verses, and with "Poetry" they appeared as *Poems* by O. W. Holmes, late in 1836. Hence in September, 1836, less than a year after his return from Paris resolved to devote himself to medicine, young Holmes was reading proof for two publications, one a prize medical essay, the other a volume of poems. The medical essay won him membership in the most active group of medical thinkers in Boston, the Boston Society for Medical Improvement. But he gave more attention to the format of his book of poems, indicating that what had been intended as his valedictory to verse-writing was anything but that.

The long poem "Poetry" was placed first, with a dedication to his brother-in-law, the Reverend Charles Upham, and with a prose preface, most of which was retained in later editions (15). The poem was in heroic couplets, as was to be expected of an author who acknowledged the influence of Pope and Goldsmith; the subject, *ars poetica*, was likewise conventionally eighteenth-century, as was the subtitle, "A Metrical Essay." Holmes noted that the poem, "being written for public delivery, required more variety than is commonly demanded in metrical essays." He got variety by dividing the poem into five sections and into irregular groups within the sections; by enlivening "Martial Poetry" with his ringing lines "Old Ironsides"; by elegiac stanzas—one on "the calm, chaste scholar" (Charles Channing Emerson, younger brother of Ralph Waldo, who had died May 6, 1836) and the other the tender lines in memory of his "dear friend" James Jackson, the brilliant medical student who had died on his return from Paris in 1834. The most personal grief was expressed for his sister Mary, lines which were later published separately as "The Cambridge Churchyard" (5-7). Although the personal passages set these lines off from being merely conventional graveyard poetry, the most originality appeared in the witty warnings to young maidens that the melancholy and pallid cheeks of "pseudo-poets" came not so much from genius as from "dull disease." The humor of the symptoms of pallor and hectic flush more probably indicating "pulmonary disease" than love's melancholy was appropriately conveyed more sharply in the printed note than in the verses.

This metrical essay for Phi Beta Kappa was Holmes's chief venture in verse for Harvard during his first year home, but he also composed and sang a "Song for the Centennial Celebration of Harvard College" on September 8. His respected medical professor Dr. Jacob Bigelow was responsible for his being lured into this further deviation from a narrow path of medical study. In 1837, Phi Beta Kappa at Harvard was after him again, this time for a poem for the dinner at which Emerson gave his famous address *The American Scholar,* called by Holmes "our intellectual Declaration of Independence." Holmes's contribution was a drinking song, "A Song of Other Days" (41-42). "The gray-haired sage," "Wisdom's self," "The Grecian's mound" were cited only to reenforce "Man wants but little drink below, / But wants that little strong." The range and poise of the young performer must have impressed Emerson, for he recommended him as a lyceum lecturer, an increasingly popular and remunerative field which both men, in distinctly different ways, were instrumental in developing. By the end of 1837, Holmes was offering two lectures, one as conventional as "Poetry," on English versification; the other, on cities, leaned heavily on his European travels. The honor of being elected a member of the American Academy of Arts and Sciences (located in Boston) in January, 1838, reflected the public approval he was gaining in both poetry and medicine.

II *Research and Teaching*

Holmes was not kept busy with patients, since a reputation for wit and poetry has never been known to increase a doctor's practice. He was pointing his studies toward research and teaching, and in 1837 he was busy preparing two more medical essays, both of which won Boylston prizes. The first came again from an outside suggestion: a study of intermittent fever (malaria) in New England. Such a study the Massachusetts Medical Society had undertaken in 1834, but had dropped because of insufficient information. Holmes ingeniously set himself to find the information he needed: besides sending out questions to doctors in different regions, he made inquiries through friends like Phineas Barnes in Maine and Dr. Parsons in Providence, and through family acquaintances. Also he toiled through colonial records and town histories, although so many records were kept by ministers, that sifting doctrine for symptoms was often painful; he admitted he had consulted only "some few ecclesiastical papers, sermons, and similar treatises of Cotton Mather, which being more likely to cause a fever than mention one, I left to some future investigator."[1]

Holmes's answer to the Boylston Prize Question "To what extent, and in what places has Intermittent Fever been indigenous in New England?" was an essay based on painstaking investigation which reached logical and careful conclusions. The praise it won in its own day was justified; as recently as 1945, it was called "the best regional history of malaria thus far written."[2] The other study, an essay on neuralgia, won the prize more for clear, vigorous presentation than for original research. It was natural that Holmes should publicize his three prizes in two years by publishing the essays together in 1838, wisely placing the study of intermittent fever first. Although patients were not many, he was occupied with giving reports at the Boston Society for Medical Improvement and with tending cases at the Boston Dispensary. He also wrote some vigorous suggestions for improving facilities, procedure, and personnel at that charitable institution.

In 1838, Holmes had his first experience of teaching when he joined Dr. Jacob Bigelow and two other doctors in forming the Tremont Medical School. Designed to offer experience in dissecting and clinical study to supplement the lectures at the Harvard Medical School, it maintained a library and clinic at 35 Tremont Row, to which address Holmes moved in 1839. In July, 1838, Dartmouth appointed him Professor of Anatomy and Physiology in the medical college in Hanover, New Hampshire; his work was to include giving lectures for fourteen weeks in the autumn and the replacing in the anatomical museum of specimens the retiring professor had owned personally and removed. Although the salary was dependent upon the number of students enrolled, and was under $500 each of the two years he lectured there, it was steady employment which required study and preparation of specimens for the museum.

But poetry was still mixed with medicine: in 1838, the Boston Society for Medical Improvement asked for and received a poem from him for its anniversary; his opening performance at Dartmouth was not as medical lecturer but as Phi Beta Kappa poet at the commencement exercises on July 24, 1839. Like his poem at his own commencement, this one came as welcome relief to an audience wearied by long orations; as a result, it received loud applause and extravagant praise. But Holmes called it "a slipshod lay" and only three parts of it were allowed magazine publication, four years later.[3]

Preparation of his new lectures and specimens and the composition of the Dartmouth poem added to his regular duties during 1838 and 1839, but he found time to help his former teacher Dr. Jacob Bigelow publish an American revision of the Englishman Marshall Hall's *Principles of the Theory and Practice of Medicine*, which went to press after he had gone to give his Dartmouth lectures in the autumn of 1839. Holmes was familiar with the book because his Paris teacher Louis had asked his help in making some of the material available to him for his teaching, and he had met and dined with the author when he had visited Louis in Paris. Early in the autumn of 1839, before Holmes left for Dartmouth, another offer, the chair of surgery at the University of Maryland, had tempted him. His quickness of mind and speech and his eager response to each new stimulus made him want to accept both offers; but graver, more experienced men warned him against attempting too much, and he heeded the warnings. He may have been unduly eager at this time because he was courting Amelia Lee Jackson, the daughter of Judge Charles Jackson and the niece and cousin of the James Jacksons whom he had studied under and with, and whom he admired as brilliant examples of his profession.

Before Holmes returned to Dartmouth in the autumn of 1840 to give his second and last term of lectures there, he was married to Amelia Jackson. The marriage took place in King's Chapel, Boston, on June 15, 1840, and Judge Jackson gave the couple a house at 8 Montgomery Place, which was their home for the next eighteen years. Holmes was past thirty, his bride twenty-two; like his mother, she was a woman of taste and gracious dignity who won the "affectionate approbation" of friends and family. The children of the marriage were three. The eldest was Oliver Wendell Holmes, Jr., born March 8, 1841—the only child who outlived his father and who lived to an even greater age; he was ninety-four when he died on October 7, 1935, to his father's eighty-five when he died October 7, 1894. Even before his father's death he was making Oliver Wendell Holmes a name distinguished for brilliant legal writings and superior jurisprudence; in 1931, he could shake his fist at his father's portrait in playful challenge that his ninetieth birthday had been celebrated with more resounding world-wide acclaim than his father's eightieth.

The second child, a daughter named Amelia Jackson after her mother, was born October 20, 1843. She married Turner Sargent in May, 1871, and they lived near her parents in Boston save for travels abroad. She was often with her parents after her husband died in April, 1877, especially after her mother's memory began to fade in 1878. In 1886, Amelia traveled to England and France with her father, and she sold her house to come and live with him after her mother died in 1888. She could not give her father her comforting companionship long, for she died in April, 1889. The third and last child, Edward Jackson, was born October 17, 1846. Trained to the law, he was married to Henrietta Goddard Wigglesworth in 1870, but he suffered severely from asthma, and died in April, 1884. He left one son, also Edward Jackson Holmes, the only lineal descendant of the third generation.[4]

Since Holmes resigned his professorship at Dartmouth after the term of 1840, and refused other offers outside Boston, he must have been able to support his growing family by fees from patients, from consultations which other doctors were increasingly demanding, and from lecturing. To his lectures on English versification and on cities he had added one on national prejudices. He continued to accede to requests for poems on medical or academic anniversaries, but his chief professional work during his first years as a family man in Boston was preparing a series of three lectures in which he exposed medical quackeries. The lectures were announced for early 1842 by the Society for the Diffusion of Useful Knowledge, a group of men who had attained positions of importance in many fields and who were more vigorous than the elaborate name would indicate.

Exposing quackeries appealed to the tendency of Holmes the satirist to ridicule human gullibility; it also implemented his characteristic search for *the true*, supported by observation, as opposed to *the false*, based on tradition and authority. The Royal Touch for scrofula, Berkeley's tar-water, and Perkins' metallic-tractors were "cures" far enough in the past to be discredited and to be acceptable subjects for ridicule. But when in his last lecture Holmes came to homeopathy, he aroused antagonists who were still following the theories of Samuel Hahnemann. Holmes presented the homeopathic theory of "like cures like" with incisive clarity, revealing the lack of evidence of cures as well as the lack of logical connection between different principles laid down. His conclusion was eloquent: "the pretended science" was a "mingled mass of perverse ingenuity, of tinsel erudition, of imbecile credulity, and of artful misrepresentation, too often mingled in practice, if we may trust the authority of its founder, with heartless and shameless imposition" (IX, 101). Holmes's close was confident: "I have lifted my voice against this lifeless delusion, rolling its shapeless bulk into the path of a noble science it is too weak to strike, or to injure." That he was over-confident and that "the shapeless bulk" continued to show life were evident by the attacks he had to return to; in 1891, in the preface to his volume of *Medical Essays,* he concluded: "Homœopathy has proved lucrative, and so long as it continues to be so will surely exist,—as surely as astrology, palmistry, and other methods of getting a living out of the weakness and credulity of mankind and womankind."[5]

The eloquent passion of the closing paragraphs of his lecture is only one reason why "Homoeopathy and Its Kindred Delusions" is probably the most pertinent for the lay reader of any of Holmes's medical essays today. The intellectual and psychological approach to human susceptibility to delusion in matters of magic cures, with carefully documented examples of how people have been persuaded to belief and stimulated to passionate defense, is as salutary today as it was in 1842. Unfortunately our scientific age offers more widely advertised opportunities for fads of diet and magic medicines than his historical and contemporary views could muster. Holmes made it easy for his readers to share his objective approach by beginning with some monstrous delusions of the past and by giving startling concrete illustrations. That "a large number of cures were due solely to nature" was a conclusion he had learned in Boston from his teacher Dr. Jacob Bigelow, the author of *Self-Limiting Diseases,* and then had learned again in Paris; he had had opportunities to observe its truth in both cities. That point proved a powerful wedge to dislodge statistics and testimonials.

He noted how many testimonials came from clergymen and ladies, this particular fad being "not the first or last hobby-horse they rode furiously." Ridiculing high-sounding but meaningless titles, he pointed out that a famous name should not count unless its fame had been gained in medical research. Today we are constantly being warned against trusting names and degrees; both may be worthless in the connection specified. Holmes's repetition of the "Infinitesimal Globule" of homeopathy made it as effectively absurd as his statement that the three independent truths of homeopathy "are about as remote from each other as the discovery of the law of gravitation, the invention of printing, and that of the mariner's compass." He cited an actual example from a French encyclopedia of medical sciences of April, 1840, to illustrate how elaborate polysyllables and meaningless titles may be used to clothe an absurdity:

"Manual of HYDROSUDOPATHY, or the Treatment of Diseases by Cold Water, etc., etc., by Dr. Bigel, Physician of the School of Strasburg, Member of the Medico-Chirurgical Institute of Naples, of the Academy of St. Petersburg,—Assessor of the College of the Empire of Russia, Physician of his late Imperial Highness the Grand Duke Constantine, Chevalier of the Legion of Honor, etc." (IX, 99).

The ability, illustrated here, to stand off and to see absurdity with a poise of intellect that enjoys the clear light thrown by comedy kept Holmes from ever being a dedicated crusader. He continued to expose the abuses of homeopathy whenever they came to his attention, but his quick, inquiring mind was soon caught by a more shocking indication of harmful ignorance in medical study and practice.

This time he was aroused by the reports being presented by colleagues in the Boston Society for Medical Improvement during 1842 on the possibility that the deadly disease of puerperal fever was carried to the mothers of babies by attending doctors and nurses. The evidence collected pointed to contagion; hence heavy responsibility was laid on the doctors themselves for the fatal outbreaks of the disease that could be counted. On January 23, 1843, Dr. John Jackson requested that the Society continue to investigate "the probability of physicians communicating" the fever from one patient to another. The next three weeks must have been busy ones for Holmes as he traced the history of the disease through records published here and abroad and made inquiries among individual doctors. On February 13, 1843, he presented before the society an answer that was acclaimed a hundred years later as, at the time it was delivered, "the most important contribution made in America to the advancement of medicine."[6] This paper, "The Contagiousness of Puerperal Fever," was often passionately eloquent, but its statements were supported and its arguments logical. The doctors who heard it wanted it published, and it appeared in the issue for April, 1843, of the magazine the society published for one year only, *New England Quarterly Journal of Medicine and Surgery*. Holmes got a few offprints to send to friends; but the small circulation of the magazine in which it appeared, combined with the paper's steadily increasing renown for content and style, has made the first printing of this essay the most sought-after American treasure of any medical collection.

Holmes's conclusions, without his powerful testimony of cases and his eloquence, were summarized in a two-page abstract in the *American Journal of the Medical Sciences* for July, 1843, and it aroused a wide response. But it was not until after the leading obstetricians in this country, Dr. Hugh L. Hodge and Dr. Charles D. Meigs of Philadelphia, had published in 1852 and 1853 separate essays ridiculing and rejecting the idea that medical attendants were guilty of spreading the fatal disease, that Holmes reprinted the essay in 1855 with additional references and cases to dispose of the defense of Hodge and Meigs and with an introductory note to the medical profession, especially to medical students. The opposition was silenced by 1857, and the idea of contagion causing the shocking deaths of new mothers was accepted in the United States, as it had been earlier in England. This milestone in the discovery of infection was achieved in this country chiefly on account of "the masterly essay of Dr. Holmes."[7]

In this essay and in the preparation of it for reprinting may be observed the cogency of Holmes's thinking in controversy and the skill with which he employs his weapons of ridicule and eloquence. He lines up the affirmative against the negative—the theory of contagion based on careful records against the defense of authority and the inexplicable by Hodge and Meigs. Hodge insists on "the value and dignity of our profession" and dismisses the proposal "that you can ever convey, in any possible manner, a horrible virus, so destructive in its effects, and so mysterious in its operations as that attributed to puerperal fever." Meigs is more insulting and more openly discards statistics for superstition: "I prefer to attribute them [epidemic deaths in a single place under one physician] to accident, or Providence, of which I can form a conception, rather than to a contagion of which I cannot form any clear idea, at least as to this particular malady."

These excerpts made by Holmes emphasize the lack of scientific curiosity of his opponents, and they also sharpen the effect of the rational evidence Holmes presents. He brings out the awful necessity of searching out cause rather than remedy: "I had rather rescue one mother from being poisoned by her attendants than claim to have saved forty out of fifty patients to whom I had carried the disease" (IX, 106). He writes with poignant compassion: "No man makes a quarrel with me over the counterpane that covers a mother, with her new-born infant at her breast. . . . I am too much in earnest for either humility or vanity, but I do entreat those who hold the keys of life and death to listen to me also for this once. I ask no personal favor; but I beg to be heard in behalf of the women whose lives are at stake, until some stronger voice shall plead for them" (IX, 110, 127).

Toward the end his eloquence is moving: "There is no tone deep enough for regret, and no voice loud enough for warning. . . . God forbid that any member of the profession to which she trusts her life, doubly precious at that eventful period, should hazard it negligently, unadvisedly, or selfishly." But he closes on the rigorous note of the scientist: he states eight rules the practitioner owes it to society to follow and he strengthens previous evidence by citing authorities between 1843 and 1855, which support the theory of contagion. Only in the final paragraph which notes added evidence does Holmes shift to his characteristic comic tone: he quotes Dr. Hodge's saying that the evidence of a single practitioner having an epidemic among his patients "has been exceedingly overrated," and then reduces it to absurdity by citing figures in many cities. "The number of them might be greater, but, ' 'tis enough, 'twill serve,' in Mercutio's modest phrase" (IX, 172).

"The Contagiousness of Puerperal Fever" was issued in 1861 as it was printed in 1855 in the first volume collecting Holmes's medical writings. The title, *Currents and Counter-Currents in Medical Science,* was that of an address he had delivered before the Massachusetts Medical Society on May 26, 1860. This address was also exploratory and controversial; he attacked the too-free use of remedies—overdosing—instead of search for the causes of the disease: "if the whole materia medica, *as now used,* could be sunk to the bottom of the sea, it would be all the better for mankind,—and all the worse for the fishes" (IX, 202-3). Indignant medical men present succeeded in getting a vote passed which implied censure of the speaker by disclaiming agreement; but by this time Holmes was hardened to professional attacks from those entrenched behind tradition and ignorance. He therefore published his three most controversial essays under the title of the one which had stirred the most recent attacks. There were seven essays in the volume, two reviews previously published in magazines and two addresses, besides these three medical essays under discussion. In all the reprintings of "The Contagiousness of Puerperal Fever"—1855, 1861, 1883 (in *Medical Essays 1842-1882*), and in the Riverside Edition in 1895[8]—Holmes pointed out that the original essay was not changed; the only additions were the mounting evidence of contagion and his sharper warnings to the medical profession of the terrible responsibility it had to bear if this doctrine was ignored.

Another notable contribution to medical history was made by Holmes in November, 1846, when he suggested the name that was ultimately accepted to designate the use of sulphuric ether to render a patient insensible to pain during an operation. W. T. G. Morton used this method with a patient in an operation performed in the Massachusetts General Hospital on October 16, 1846, and in another the day following. The surgeon was the famous Dr. John Collins Warren, and the occasion was one of the most famous in recorded medical history. Holmes was not present at either operation because his third child was born on October 17. But on November 21 he wrote to Morton:

> Everybody wants to have a hand in a great discovery. All I will do is to give a hint or two as to names—or the name—to be applied to the state produced and the agent.
> The state should, I think be called "Anaesthesia." This signifies insensibility—more particularly (as used by Linnaeus and Cullen) to objects of touch. (See Good—Nosology, p. 259.)
> The adjective will be "Anaesthetic." Thus we might say the state of Anaesthesia, or the anaesthetic state. . . .
>
> . . . .
>
> I would have a name pretty soon, and consult some accomplished scholar, . . . before fixing upon the terms, which *will be repeated by the tongues of every civilized race of mankind.*[9]

It is needless to say at this date that Holmes's term *anaesthesia* was accepted instead of *Letheon.*

III   *Occasional Poems*

Although the years from 1838 to 1846 were filled for Holmes with lecturing, research, and publishing—to say nothing of marriage and a growing family of three children—his previous success as an occasional poet brought him many requests for public appearances. In 1846 when a London edition of his poems was being prepared with the cooperation of his American publishers, nine poems were at hand to be added to the first edition of 1836, five of them written for specific occasions and delivered or sung at them, with one exception, by Holmes. The other four were obviously requested by editors. Two of them were conventional gift-book verses; one was topical. "The Steamboat" (28) had appeared appropriately in *The Knickerbocker* for March, 1839; for, published in New York, it was close to the Hudson River where the invention had made its trial run. The fourth deserves mention because it gives evidence of the comic play Holmes was now enjoying even in the midst of conventional sentiment. "The Parting Word" (40-41) appeared in *The Western Messenger* for May, 1838, a magazine Holmes's classmate and fellow-poet, the Reverend James Freeman Clarke, was interested in starting in Louisville, Kentucky, where he was preaching. In contrast to the title and the lachrymose parting of the sailor from his love in the first two stanzas and the last, the six stanzas between give amusing scenes where "Men and devils both contrive / Traps for catching girls alive; / Eve was duped, and Helen kissed,— / How, oh how, can you resist?"

Of the strictly occasional new poems, a "Song Written for the Dinner given Charles Dickens by the Young Men of Boston" (33), on February 1, 1842, was set to music by two composers; it was apparently sung by Holmes at the dinner. It offered tuneful compliment to an author who, like Shakespeare, was as much our delight as England's; but a hint of satire lurks in our weeping "Alike o'er Juliet's storied tomb / And Nelly's nameless grave." In November, 1842, Holmes sent to New York a "Song" which was sung by another at the "Anniversary Dinner of the New York Mercantile Library Association to which Ladies were invited"; later it was entitled "Song for a Temperance Dinner" (42). As was to be expected from a poet who had so often celebrated wine and the ensuing conviviality, Holmes's approach to the pale wife waiting for her drunken husband to come home was original: his solution was to invite the ladies to come to drink too—"So, room for the Girls!"

The tuneful gaiety of this poem was turned to sharper comment in a poem about the invasion from Germany of transcendental philosophy, which Holmes suspected of being as alluring and as false as Hahnemann's homeopathy. "An After-Dinner Poem (Terpsichore)" (54-57) was written for the Phi Beta Kappa Dinner at Harvard on August 24, 1843. The classical goddess of the dance and the satiric touches were appropriately phrased in the heroic couplet, with an invocation to his usual "reluctant Muse," who was to "Bound to the footlights for thy brief display,

/ One zephyr step, and then dissolve away!" He lists the fields he has no time for: Fancy, Wit, Pathos, Mirth, Satire. But he does survey with sharp detail and concrete figure the opportunities for the latter as in "Poems that shuffle with superfluous legs / A blindfold minuet over addled eggs." The "Mesmeric pamphlets" and "homœopathic pills" are echoes of his essay of the year before, *Homœopathy and Its Kindred Delusions.* Another item from the year before is the mention of Dickens, for whom he had written and sung a welcome, but whose overenthusiastic American reception he scores lightly: "While the great Feasted views with silent glee / His scattered limbs in Yankee fricassee."

His sharpest attack, however, is upon transcendental philosophy. The "weak eclectic" is symbolized by his "German-silver spoon," and the romantic and the transcendentalist are asking impossible questions of Earth and Time.

> Here babbling "Insight" shouts in Nature's ears
> His last conundrum on the orbs and spheres;
> There Self-inspection sucks its little thumb,
> With "Whence am I?" and "Wherefore did I come?"
> Deluded infants! Will they ever know
> Some doubts must darken o'er the world below,
> Though all the Platos of the nursery trail
> Their "clouds of glory" at the go-cart's tail?

The attack is brought artistically within the realm of the dancing goddess by the diction at the end:

> Too blest by fortune if the passing day
> Adorn thy bosom with its frail bouquet,
> But oh, still happier if the next forgets
> Thy daring steps and dangerous pirouettes!

Although the writers for *The Dial* and the men of Concord were apparently quite undisturbed by these lines—if they heard or read them—Holmes was on his guard when he offered them to Rufus Griswold for *Graham's Monthly Magazine* in New York. He wrote the editor that "for me it was remarkably happy . . . it has more point in it than most of the things of the kind I have done lately. . . . Are you afraid of a hint at repudiation in it?"[10] That Holmes wanted publication outside of Boston was implied by his mentioning that he was offering it to Griswold rather than to the editor of

Godey's Lady's Book. The alert social sense which had become
sensitive during the years of his father's trouble in Cambridge
made him aware of a danger of hurt feelings among his targets.
The title *Terpsichore* was used when it appeared in *Graham's
Magazine* for January, 1844 (XXV, 10-11).

The two poems Holmes wrote for occasions in 1844 found him
on safer ground. The "Wendell" in his name caused the town of
Pittsfield to invite this grandson of the Jacob Wendell who had
bought 24,000 acres there in 1735 to deliver some verses at its
jubilee on August 23. He accepted and prefaced his "Lines"
(33-34) by remarks showing he was at least "allied to it by
hereditary relation." The quick verses proved an acceptable mixture of homecoming sentiment and colloquial diction that invited
the comfortable laughter of recognition. Six days later, on August
29, his thirty-fifth birthday, he recited "Verses for After-Dinner"
(36-37) for the Phi Beta Kappa Society at Harvard. He played it
safe with comic reference to "the cannibal president" who called
him up too often. In rollicking anapests he developed a fable of
the fishes, in which a Flounder, Sculpin, and Pickerel were
brought in to feed on each other; he ended with a moral in the
last stanza:

> And thus, O survivor, whose merciless fate
> Is to take the next hook with the president's bait,
> You are lost while you snatch from the end of the line
> The morsel he rent from this bosom of mine!

He was let off from performing for Phi Beta Kappa the next
year, but on December 22, 1845, he read "The Pilgrim's Vision"
(26-28) at the celebration of the 225th Anniversary of the
Pilgrims' landing at Plymouth. The "grim old soldier-saint" gave
his own version of American history to the "Pilgrim-child": from
the fighting to victory over the Indians and the "Mistress of the
Seas" to the spreading out over the continent, Faith had given
the enduring legend "Here was the Pilgrim's land!" The concrete pictures, the rapid accent, and the dramatic scenes made
it effectively suited to the occasion.[11]

Holmes's next appearance as occasional poet was markedly
less successful; at least the poem is when read today. It illustrates
all too well his remark that many of his "lesser poems were
written for meetings more or less convivial, and must of course

show something like the fire-work frames on the morning of July 5th" (26, "Letter from the Author to the Publishers," 1849). The title implied the irony: "A Modest Request Complied with after the Dinner at President Everett's Inauguration" (37-40). The date was April 30, 1846, and the by now familiar opening showed him being asked to perform. The best lines were the ones Holmes put in the letter to him, setting forth the reasons he was summoned:

> Yours is the art, by native genius taught,
> To clothe in eloquence the naked thought;
> Yours is the skill its music to prolong
> Through the sweet effluence of mellifluous song;
> Yours the quaint trick to cram the pithy line
> That cracks so crisply over bubbling wine;
>
> . . . .
>
> We—that is, I and all your numerous friends—
> Expect from you—your single self a host—
> A speech, a song, excuse me, *and* a toast;
> Nay, not to haggle on so small a claim,
> A few of each, or several of the same.

The irony of *modest* being applied to a request for a speech, a song, and a toast was unfortunately carried over into the performance. Instead of offering eloquence, wit, and melody, Holmes's poem was self-conscious and wordy.

The other occasional poem of 1846 was different. Called "A Rhymed Lesson (Urania)" (43-54), the classic title in parentheses, the couplet form, and the didactic tone touched by the satiric are like his long poem of 1843, "An After-Dinner Poem (Terpsichore)." It was delivered before the Boston Mercantile Library Association on October 14, 1846. As at the two commencements, the audience had to wait impatiently through a long-winded oration of more than an hour for the poet. Many were sad to see the poet skip parts of his manuscript to bring his prepared poem to a needed brevity. Holmes's success as an occasional poet derived partly from his being acutely aware of his audience—sometimes too aware, as he would often stop for comment. He did that here, noting that many came only to be amused, and he promised them "A smile awaits them ere my song is through!" But he also warned "While my gay stanza pleased the banquet's lords, / The soul within was tuned to deeper chords!"

The "deeper chords" he struck against the dark creed of the Calvinists, which he discarded in favor of a God of love, a God that granted human beings Thought, Conscience, and Will to use for their own growth and happiness as much as for God's glory. His own departure from creed and doctrine was emphasized by his use of *Urania*, the pagan goddess of spiritual love. Christian tolerance was made vivid by scenes from a Sunday morning in Boston, where bells summoned worshippers to various churches (bells and churches were identified by Holmes in notes in all the printings). In contrast to the Puritan's bitterness against Roman Catholics, he presented Irish Nora tenderly and advised: "Have thine own faith,—but hope and pray for all!" In a sharper tone he warned against the crusading reformer, the delusion of the goddess Progress, and the temptation to find a quick way to recognition by being *ultra*. Ridicule of our frantic search for a "native bard" was only tinged with satire: "The babe of nature in the 'giant West,' / Must be of course her biggest and her best." He gave his vote for the importance to the poet of the heart's intensity as against mere region, but he concluded rather illogically with concrete detail of the "three hills" of Boston. Their value lay, however, in the lesson of Virtue and Patriot Valor lent them by history—not in "the odd notion that the poet's dreams / Grow in the ratio of his hills and streams." This poem came too late in 1846 for the London edition of Holmes's poems; but, published separately in Boston in October, it passed to a third edition before the year was out, indicating that its satiric touches and topical comment won a wider audience than had waited for its first delivery, or had heard it without omissions the next week at the Cambridge Lyceum.

I have given in some detail Holmes's poetical as well as his medical achievements of this period because his medical activities were important for their own sake and because the place he was taking as poet and thinker was important in relation to the position he developed later. Thus it is startling to discover that his position was so objectionable to James Russell Lowell that he wrote Holmes decrying his conservative stand, his persistently comic tone, and his failure to take a stand on the Mexican War and on slavery. Lowell and his first wife were intensely stirred by these last two problems. The letter of Lowell does not survive, but its contents may be inferred from the long reply Holmes wrote on November 29, 1846, which was published by Morse (I, 295-303) and still survives in manuscript. In this letter Holmes took up the "Causes" Lowell had blamed him for giving "many shrewd rubs." *War* came first, and Holmes found it hateful for settling national quarrels, even if he still saw beauty in the heroism and devotion of the Revolutionary heroes. *Slavery* he dismissed as so much talked about as to make it pointless for him to denounce it before such an audience. *Temperance* he claimed some credit for supporting by not publishing one or two of his favorite poems which extolled the joys of wine, by his "Song for a Temperance Dinner," and by taking a lower rent for his mother's shop on Long Wharf to keep it from being a rum shop. The *claims of the poor* and *reforms* and *reformers* were the last items in Lowell's indictment; and Holmes declared he was eager for practical deeds rather than emotional embroilment. He had ridiculed the reformer and the seeker for the *ultra* only as they enjoyed being personally conspicuous. He rejected any suggestion he would expurgate conscience, and he pointed out not only the importance he gave it as a guide but also his stress on love and on tolerance. He replied to the charge of being a conservative by mentioning how far to the left of the most liberal he was among medical thinkers. He admitted he might appear "lazy, or indifferent, or timid," but he was by no means chained to the status quo as opposed to reason.

This was not the first or the last time that Holmes's sallies angered the zealous. Because Lowell and Holmes are so often placed together as examples of the New England "Brahmins" (whom Holmes named), their differences as they were becoming recognized as writers deserve full notice, especially since Lowell used Holmes's devices of dialect and comedy in his *Biglow Papers* with such success. The defense Holmes offered in his letter explains why he was never an abolitionist: he thought it humanly impossible to exterminate slavery. The danger he feared was disunion, and the abolitionists seemed to him to be promoting that. After answering specific charges, Holmes stressed the moral lessons that were often taught by his comic scenes and diction: "one set of critics proscribe me for being serious and another for being gay."

As an artist he adorned scenes of common life with "colors borrowed from the imagination and the feelings." His satire was kindly and aimed only "at the excesses of well-meaning people." Although he would reflect seriously on criticisms, he had to follow his natural bent: "I shall always be pleased rather to show what is beautiful in the life around me than be pitching into giant vices, against which the acrid pulpit and the corrosive newspaper will always anticipate the gentle poet." That this attitude was persistent was clear in the different phrasing of his later years: "I prefer to take a good bite out of life, sunny side up; after that, let in the pigs." He reserved the right to his theory of life, of art, of his own existence and relations: "to improve and please my fellow-men after my own fashion." With him life and social relations were always close to art; *improve* was increasingly put before *please*. Never again did a published work of Holmes reveal such banal frivolity as his poem "A Modest Request" of 1846. The satiric note directed against such features of contemporary life as transcendentalism, the wholesale swallowing of Dickens, and the Abolition movement gave way—with a rare exception or two—to healthy laughter at what fools we mortals be and to an occasional passionate defense of truth as threatened by entrenched error.

Other illuminating comments about himself as poet were made in letters from Holmes to Emerson in 1847, to Griswold in 1842, and to Lowell in 1848 and 1849 after he had sent Holmes copies of his *Fable for Critics* and of his *Vision of Sir Launfal* (Morse, 107-9; 109-11). Holmes repeated: "I can't be one of the 'earnest' folks if I try ever so hard." His reliance on the heroic couplet he phrased "such an old-fashioned versifying squaretoes as myself"; but he defended "the old square-toed heroic" and retorted upon "the rattlety-bang sort of verse in which you have indulged." Holmes did rely on the heroic couplet for long poems; but his most famous poems were the short lyrics which, as he confessed to Clarke, he had to labor over to make them songs. Holmes was inclined to boast that Poe had taught him to scan the effective short-line form of "The Last Leaf," but this statement fitted the image of reluctant poet he fancied for public use. Poe's admiration was genuine, because he apparently asked for copies of recent poems in 1846, especially of *Urania*,[12] but there is no record of his comment. In 1842, Rufus Griswold had included fifteen of Holmes's poems, with a brief biography Holmes wrote for him, in *The Poets and Poetry of America*, and the letter Holmes wrote thanking him revealed a concern with verse that was in direct contradiction to his repeated picture of one lured into writing poetry only because of friendly acquiescence to the demands of friends. To him, Griswold's volume represented "one of the happiest literary undertakings we have seen on this side of the water," and he hoped it would become "our poetical gospel."[13]

A letter to Emerson (thanking him for his *Poems* [1847]) strengthens the image of a Holmes who had ideas about poetry and the importance of rhythm to its success. He found it odd that one as conscious of nature's rhythm as Emerson "should sometimes undervalue it as a means of expression." He gave high praise to the "wild strawberry flavor" of the nature detail, but he was as frank as he had been with Lowell on the points he disagreed with: "I have nothing to do with thoughts that roll beyond a certain width of orbit."[14] Emerson's "blue empyrean" offered Holmes chiefly vagueness, perhaps dangerous distortion. These serious remarks of a practicing poet suggest that Holmes was like Gifted Hopkins, the pseudo-poet he gently laughed at in *The Guardian Angel*: "He had tasted the blood of his own rhymes; and when a poet gets as far as that, it is like wringing the bag of exhilarating gas from the lips of a fellow sucking at it, to drag his piece away from him" (VI, 228).

From 1836 through 1846, it is possible to trace two paths Holmes actively followed: the path of medical research and publication, and the path of poetry, down which he moved with outward reluctance but gay competence, developing some satiric form and content and some firm standards of poetic performance. These paths joined in many poems he wrote for medical meetings and dinners. Although most of these were not published because of professional accent and diction, two were included in the 1849 Boston edition of his poems and also in the Riverside edition: "The Stethoscope Song" and "Extracts from a Medical Poem: The Stability of Science." The latter was read at a meeting of the Massachusetts Medical Society on May 31, 1843; it included another tribute to the late Dr. James Jackson, "And love renewing kept him ever young," as well as a figure of Science like a lighthouse ever radiant and firm against "fluttering folly" (61-62). The earlier (1838?), "The Stethoscope Song: A Professional Ballad" (60-61), has a rapid movement and a gay mockery that make it worthy to rank with his early comic songs. Its subject makes it certainly a product of the months after his return from Paris: his self-important hero is impressing all with his stethoscope and his experience with its use under Louis. Unfortunately an intruding spider and two flies have rendered its diagnoses false and alarming. The use of French and of medical terms heightens the comedy; the particular aspect of Holmes's laughter that makes it contagious and winning is that the "new-fashioned toys" he ridicules when overvalued are his own. He was as alert to the *ultra* and its dangers in himself and in his profession as in transcendentalism and abolitionism, and he could point them out with the poise of comedy and the rhythm of verse.

IV   *Harvard Professor and Lecturer*

In April, 1847, Holmes was invited to be a member of the faculty of the Harvard Medical School; and in November as Parkman Professor of Anatomy and Physiology, he began the lectures which he gave for thirty-five years. In tribute to his reputation as a speaker, his lectures were always set at the most trying hour: at first, at one o'clock, after the students had been listening to lectures during an entire morning; after 1851, the hour was changed to twelve, but the period was still the most difficult during which to hold the attention of weary, hungry young men. All evidence points to Holmes's success in holding and enlightening his audience; he emphasized illustration, prepared specimens carefully, and trained demonstrators to work with him who were lastingly grateful for their experience. More clinical training was still offered by him and others in the Tremont Medical School, and it was taken by many students to supplement the lectures at Harvard. In 1858, the two schools were merged; but from 1847 to 1853 Holmes was an important figure in both: he acted as dean of the Harvard Medical School and as secretary of the Tremont. Professors were still paid according to the number of tickets sold for their lectures. The work of dean which Holmes assumed before lectures began in November, 1847, was largely clerical; at least the number of reports he wrote by hand of faculty schedules and students' papers is stupefying to twentieth-century officials and readers accustomed to having such drudgery performed by secretaries and typewriters.

On November 3, 1847, Holmes began a custom which was continued throughout his term of teaching; he gave an introductory lecture to which the president and the Board of Over-seers of Harvard were invited. He did not give all of these while he was teaching, but he gave a good many. He was so busy lecturing and preparing demonstrations that he refused all invitations to lecture outside; in 1848, for example, he refused to give the Phi Beta Kappa poem at Yale. His first lecture remains of importance for its serious approach to thorough training of students and to the maintenance of standards in this country. Earlier he had attended a meeting to start the establish-ment of the American Medical Association, and he spoke with eager hope of what such an organization might achieve; at the request of the students this lecture was printed.

Outsiders like the liberal clergyman Theodore Parker and the musician John Dwight Sullivan asked permission to attend his medical lectures regularly, and received it. Another who asked to attend medical lectures at Harvard in December, 1847, was denied admission: Harriot Hunt wrote Holmes stressing her serious desire to receive more instruction, and her maturity. Holmes wrote President Everett a letter to accompany her application, in which he approved her request and cited as precedent the brilliant lectures by a woman he had heard in Paris. President Everett and the Board of Overseers decided, however, that "promiscuous attendance of the Sexes on the anatomical lectures" could not be allowed.

Holmes had more success in arranging opportunities for the dissection he had found so valuable in Paris; in August, 1848, he gave the City of Boston a bond of $5,000 in return for permission to use the bodies of certain persons buried at public expense. Three conditions, however, were attached to this permis-sion: they were to be used only for promoting anatomical science; they were not to be used in a way to outrage public feeling; the remains were to be decently buried.[15] But the most spectacular corpse at the Harvard Medical School during Holmes's six years as dean was that of Dr. George Parkman, who was murdered by Professor of Chemistry John Webster on the afternoon of November 23, 1849, when he came to an appointment hoping to collect a little on the heavy debt owed him by Webster. The school was closed from November 30 to December 8 while the janitor was locating parts of Parkman's body which Webster had tried to hide or dispose of in the basement. As dean, Holmes wrote to Webster in prison to ask his advice about a temporary replacement; a permanent one became necessary after Webster was found guilty of the murder. Holmes's official notes to the president made only vague reference to the unfortunate reason a replacement was needed; he testified on both sides at the trial: as dean, for Webster's skill and faithful performance; as an anatomist, for the identification of the bones as Parkman's. In November, 1850, when the introductory lecture at Harvard Medical School was in memory of Dr. Parkman, Holmes was chosen to give it, not so much because he was Parkman Professor (Parkman's gifts had been used for buildings rather than salaries) as because he had taste and proven skill as a public speaker no matter how trying the circumstances.

In 1848, Mrs. Holmes had inherited $2,000; and with Holmes's position as medical professor and lecturer assured, and young children to rear, they decided to establish a summer home on what was left of the Wendell estate in Pittsfield. Plans for a house were decided upon, and the family went in July, 1849, to spend the first of "seven blessed summers" in Pittsfield. Added expenses in connection with a summer place immediately began to appear: horses, a barn, a carryall, fences, more help; moreover, the house cost twice as much as planned; and for these reasons "Canoe Meadow" (the name the estate had long carried) was put up for sale in May, 1856. On January 1, 1849, Holmes had notified his patients that he was giving up all private practice; he resigned from the committee for the Bolyston Prizes, and he delegated his duties as dean to a member of the Medical Faculty remaining in Boston during the summer months. Others than the children enjoyed country activities: on September 26, 1849, John Holmes wrote Lowell from Pittsfield: "I have here been robustious, laborious, an early riser, and a prodigious admirer of nature. I have chopped wood and tried to catch a pickerel, and killed a frog. . . ."[16]

Dr. Holmes's poems written for occasions in Pittsfield indicate that he also became "a prodigious admirer of nature." But his special delights were owning and driving a horse—preferably a fast one—measuring large trees, and planting an avenue of trees which still marks the approach to the house. His reputation for fast horses won him an invitation to take part in the National Horse Exhibition at Springfield, Massachusetts, on October 19, 1853. J. G. Holland's invitation to enter his "Horse with Wings" stirred Holmes to reply with the figure and a rush of puns that suggest the image he had created for his demanding public: the glancing play on word after word indicates that, however informal his personal asides in poems delivered on occasions may seem in print, they are as nothing to the fireworks which the little man discharged spontaneously.

> I am much obliged to you for the polite invitation to appear (on horseback) at the great Equestrian Banquet. I doubt not you would have plenty of nice bits, ready for the flying horse referred to, and his rider, and for aught I know a saddle—of venison may form a part of the entertainment. Unfortunately he is entered for a grand sweepstakes on the twentieth; the track running through Springfield, but the winning post in Boston. In plain English the 20th of October is the day appointed for the annual migration of the family to which the horse in question belongs from Pittsfield to its city quarters. Now my past experience has taught me that in this match against time so much weight is carried, the animal is good for nothing else during the whole week in which it takes place.
>
> If there should be any report, therefore, of trotting, running, or flying matches, please enter the following:
>
> O. W. Holmes names f.h. *Pegasus*.
> Withdrawn, pd. forfeit.[17]

The summers in Pittsfield gave Holmes an opportunity to indulge his hobby of measuring large trees and keeping records of the ones that were largest round. The Autocrat described in detail Holmes's habit of measuring with his thirty-foot tape at a height of five feet from the ground—a height determined more by Holmes's own five feet three than by sound scientific rule—all the celebrated trees he could visit, because "I have a most intense, passionate fondness for trees in general, and have had several romantic attachments to certain trees in particular" (I, 231).

The social event attended by Holmes during his stay in Pittsfield which has evoked the most literary comment was the picnic given by Dudley Field of Stockbridge on August 5, 1850.[18] He gathered the three literary figures in the vicinity: Holmes; Melville, also from Pittsfield, with his New York publisher Evert Duyckinck and with Cornelius Matthews, the editor of the latter's *Literary World;* and Hawthorne from Lenox, with his—soon Holmes's—publisher James T. Fields and his new wife Annie. The physical closeness of Hawthorne and Melville was as significant of a deep inner kinship as the meeting of Holmes with James and Annie Fields was a promise of an intimacy easily and fully expressed, which ripened during long years of sharing tastes and activities.

V Verse and Lectures

Of the many occasional poems Holmes wrote and delivered during these years a few point significantly to shifts from or echoes of the established pattern. In his verses nature had been incidental to human relations or social teachings. But occasional poems delivered in Pittsfield showed his sensitive response to the beauties of the countryside. Poems he gave at the Young Ladies' Institute on September 27, 1849, and at the Festival of St. Stephen's Parish on August 9, 1855, were published only locally. He set a higher value on two poems delivered at gatherings of the Berkshire Agricultural Society—"The Ploughman" (79-80) on October 4, 1849, and "The New Eden" (94-96) on September 16, 1854—and on the "Poem for the Dedication of the Pittsfield Cemetery" (67-89) on September 9, 1850. It was no accident that, when the editor of the *Old Farmer's Almanack* devoted the number for 1863 only to Holmes's verse, these were the poems most quoted from. Some verses of Holmes had been reprinted in the *Almanack* since the number for 1848; but when the editor wanted to feature the poetry of the popular essayist of the Breakfast-Table series and novelist in 1863, the poems of Pittsfield days offered seasonal changes aptly and melodiously recorded.

Holmes also chose lines for the *Almanack* from two other long poems of this period which were less obviously poems dealing with the countryside. On November 14, 1855, he had introduced the thirteenth annual course of lectures at the Boston Mercantile Library Association with a poem he called "The Heart's Own Secret," a poem made up of several figures who revealed pictorially and emotionally their inner dreams. The poem was not published as a whole, but parts appeared in his books from 1862 to 1891 under various titles, indicating that his psychological probing with a moral accent belonged more to an inner than to an outer image. The hearts whose secrets he sought were those of "The Old Player" (85-86); of the Banker, the Exile, the Lover, the Statesman, and the Mother; and finally "of the Stars" (307-20). In the last he outlined a union of Science with faith in God and His universe which he accepted without struggle or compromise, partly because he welcomed Science as a way to Truth, however unsettling; partly because the imaginative poet was close to the literal, fact-finding investigator.

> Maker of earth and stars! If thou hast taught
> By what thy voice hath spoke, thy hand hath wrought,
> By all that Science proves, or guesses true,
> More than thy poet dreamed, thy prophet knew,—
>
> .   .   .   .
>
> What thou shalt tell us, grant us strength to bear;
> What thou withholdest is thy single care.
>
> .   .   .   .
>
> No marbled form that sculptured truth can wear
> Vies with the image shaped in viewless air;
> And thought unfettered grows through speech to deeds
> As the broad forest marches in its seeds.
> What though we perish ere the day is won?
> Enough to see its glorious work begun!
>
> (319-20)

These were not, however, the lines Holmes chose for the *Almanack;* they noted the thistle and "the flying thistle-down."

The other long poem from which he selected lines for the 1863 *Almanack* was *Astraea,* a poem written for the Yale Phi Beta Kappa ceremony of August 14, 1850, the ceremony he had been too busy to help celebrate in 1848. The poem was published separately in 1850, but Holmes selected only parts of it for his own volumes of poetry, until the remaining lines were included in the Appendix of the Riverside edition. Lines from "Spring" (80-81) were chosen for the *Almanack;* this was the only part of *Astraea* that was not far removed from descriptive nature poetry. As in "The Secret of the Stars" many lines rejoiced in the divine mystery of nature, as Holmes saw "the trivial flourish" or "discordant strain" fading before the faith that "worlds unseen surround the worlds we know." But only in brief descriptive details of nature's seasons and triumphant trust in man's free-ranging intellect and nature's power were the two poems alike. *Astraea* (the classical goddess of justice) had the subtitle *The Balance of Illusions,* and followed the pattern of *Terpsichore* and *Urania* not only in classical title but also in form—heroic couplets arranged in sections—and in satiric comment. The *exemplum* made famous by the caustic, brilliant couplets of Dryden and Pope appeared again in "The Moral Bully" (84-85). The contempt which sharpened the details selected to etch his picture was in sharp contrast to the tender "Heart's Secret" of "The Old Player" who clung to the stage he had once adorned. He was not ridiculed but comforted: "Death only grasps; to live is to pursue,—/ Dream on! there's nothing but illusion true!"

Both these long poems revealed Holmes as a poet with polished tools which enabled him to convey mood and message vigorously: compassionate understanding of "The Old Player"; scorn of "The Moral Bully." The bully "carries but a doubtful trace / Of angel visits on his hungry face," and Holmes questioned his "right to stick us with his cutthroat terms, / And bait his homilies with his brother worms." Besides this scathing *exemplum, Astraea* took aim at the "pseudo-critic-editorial race" which owed "no allegiance but the law of place" (336)—the metropolitan New Yorkers who were beginning to look down on Boston authors. When Duyckinck protested this attack was unjustified, Holmes defended his stand as he had earlier with Lowell: his thrusts were aimed only at the false, the pretentious, and the ignorant.

From 1851 to 1856, Holmes was most active as a lyceum lecturer. The three lectures of 1841 and 1842, given in or near Boston, had been replaced by a lecture on "Medical Science as It Is or Has Been" for the 1850-51 season. The entire weeks he gave to one-night stands in New York State and New England came in March or October, just before or after his course of lectures at Harvard. In the season of 1852-53, he apparently expected to have audiences more anxious to be amused or emotionally stirred than to be instructed, for he added the topics, "Lectures and Lecturing," "The Audience," and "Love of Nature." In March and April, 1853, he gave the Lowell Institute Lectures in Boston; his subject was "English Poets of the Nineteenth Century." The audiences that gathered for the twelve lectures were so large that each lecture had to be repeated on a succeeding afternoon or evening, and even then not all who wanted to could get in. Here Holmes began the custom he used in later lectures and in the articles of his Breakfast-Table series: he capped his prose by some lines of verse, more because that was the public "dress" he was used to wearing than because he wished to exhibit his facility. The lectures were never printed, and only five of the poems were preserved (90-94). Holmes knew his own taste and method were personal rather than scholarly and sound: he ridiculed Wordsworth's attempts to escape from the "poetic diction" of Holmes's eighteenth-century masters, and he chose at random ideas or themes to illustrate, by reading from the poets.

In October and November, 1853, Holmes gave another series of lectures in Boston, this time six at the Boston Mercantile Library Association. Besides the three titles he had used for lyceum lectures of that season, he combined two Lowell Institute Lectures into "Byron and Moore," and he added "The Americanized European" and "Literary Tribunals." Holmes's list of lectures he gave from 1851 through 1854 shows eighty in his peak year, 1852-53. In March, 1854, he traveled to Haverhill, where he met Whittier and began a tender and lasting friendship; in September, 1855, he was in Louisville, Kentucky; for ten days in October, 1857, he was lecturing in Canada.[19] Then he gave it up, in spite of his love of talking and his delight in the response of audiences. The vogue of lyceum lectures was waning; to win an audience without prepossessing charm of face, figure, or voice was exhausting even to his store of quick energy; the exposures of travel and lodging increased his sufferings from asthma; and the new *Atlantic Monthly* was offering him a chance to address a wider audience without venturing away from home.

In 1858, Holmes twice expressed reactions to the career of lecturer. In the sixth paper of *The Autocrat* (I, 138-42), that gentleman held forth on the excitement of giving a new lecture and the questionable improvement after the hundredth delivery. "One learns to make the most of their strong points and to carry off their weak ones,—to take out the really good things which don't tell on the audience, and put in cheaper things that do." But the Autocrat's Landlady gave colloquial reality to the physical strain Holmes had to avoid: the lingering image of Holmes happy only in sight of the State House dome grew from a physical state rather than from a mental one.

> He was a man that loved to stick around home as much as any cat you ever see in your life. He used to say he'd as lief have a tooth pulled as go away anywheres. Always got sick, he said, when he went away, and never sick when he didn't. Pretty nigh killed himself goin' about lecterin' two or three winters,—talkin' in cold country lyceums,—as he used to say,—goin' home to cold parlors and bein' treated to cold apples and cold water, and then goin' up into a cold bed in a cold chamber, and comin' home next mornin' with a cold in his head as bad as the horse distemper.

Holmes was deeply grateful to the kind women who gave him an eiderdown comforter, a hot drink, and a cigar after the lecture; but he "preferred a natural death to puttin' himself out of the world by such violent means as lecturin'."[20]

The last lecture Holmes gave in 1855 was on December 22, at the Semi-Centennial Anniversary of the New England Society of New York; it was so unfortunate in every respect that a man less naïve in politics and less protected by admirers might have determined upon public silence—at least until antislavery agitation had subsided. He insisted that the abolitionists who were objecting to slave-owning were disloyal to the government— hence treasonable. Little wonder that the hisses drowned out the applause or that the New York newspapers were after him the next day, often with distorted versions of what he had said. Holmes's conscience would seem to have been involved since he did not alter his stand; for, in an "Ode for Washington's Birthday" (98), delivered before the Boston Mercantile Library Association in 1856, he had the Father of his country warning: "Doubt the patriot whose suggestions / Strive a nation to divide!" He looked beyond the growing furor against slavery in the North to what was to him the gravest danger—the destruction of the Union. Ironically his psychological studies of men as social beings made him more prophetic of confusions attendant upon wholesale emancipation than aware of the turbulent stirrings of his audiences. A man who shunned argument and crusades, he was venturing upon a volcano.

His failure to join the crusaders at this time did not prevent his being honored by election to the Massachusetts Historical

Society in September, 1857. His poetry had an audience in England, and in 1852, the well-known firm of Routledge brought out *The Poetical Works of Oliver Wendell Holmes* in what it announced to be the first English edition. Since there had been an edition in London in 1846, in which book publication of several poems had antedated that of the 1849 edition in Boston, this was obviously misinformation or publisher's snobbery. The sale of such a volume was promoted by what Motley had reported to Holmes from London: that Thackeray, who had been in the United States in the spring of 1853 winning his own success on the lecture platform, had heard Holmes's Lowell Lectures and had announced on his return to England that the best thing he had heard and seen in America had been Oliver Wendell Holmes.[21]

VI Harvard Poet and War Writer

The direction Holmes was taking was to make him the poet par excellence for expressing deep feelings of trust and loyalty at serious gatherings as well as gay humor at festival affairs, where he had always been noted for delivering verses made "to pop with the corks." He appreciated the serious attention he received from the critic Edwin P. Whipple. The comment Holmes welcomed began with his comic verse and emphasized that "to blend ludicrous ideas with fancy and imagination, and display in their conception and expression the same poetic qualities usually exercised in serious composition is a rare distinction." The author who more than once revealed that to make light verse sound easy required hours of toil, naturally responded to such analysis. Whipple went on to consider Holmes as "a poet of sentiment and passion. Those who know him only as a comic lyricist, as the libellous laureate of chirping folly and presumptuous egotism, would be surprised at the clear sweetness and skylark thrill of his serious and sentimental compositions."[22]

I have chosen the series of poems he wrote for his class dinners as an illustration of how successfully he played with various tones and figures upon the single string of loving loyalty. The poems of the war and other writings are included, as they were used as class poems or contributed to the mood expressed in a particular year. Although Holmes was chosen Class Poet in 1829, the poems to be considered are those he began writing for the annual class meeting in 1851, and continued to write through 1889.[23] Holmes first put these poems into the section "Poems of the Class of '29" in *Songs of Many Seasons 1862-1874*, and he added to it in the collected editions (113-48). The forty-four poems finally assembled were arranged chronologically save for the first, which was one of three Holmes offered at the class meeting in January, 1869. Called "Bill and Joe" (113-14), it had been written for the Harvard Phi Beta Kappa dinner on July 16, 1868, but the author noted it was really by and about the Class of 1829. Then the use of first names like Bill and Joe indicated a real intimacy; Clarke, Lowell, and Sargent were among the few outside the family who addressed Holmes as "Wendell." The familiar tone here was the key; with it went the temerity of the jester who approached even a tombstone with gay irreverence.

The song for 1854, "The Old Man Dreams" (115-16), exhibited another combination which Holmes achieved successfully with rare exceptions: dream and sentiment jolted into wholesome laughter by practical facts. As the poet asked for "one hour of youthful joy" and "my twentieth spring" again, the listening angel asked him if there wasn't anything on his track to hold back this return.

> "Ah, truest soul of womankind!
> Without thee what were life?
> One bliss I cannot leave behind:
> I'll take—my—precious—wife!"

Further questions revealed his "fond paternal joys," which made him want to take his girls and boys. A refrain with the required difference brightened the seventh and tenth stanzas:

> The angel took a sapphire pen
> And wrote in rainbow dew,
> *The man would be a boy again,*
> *And be a husband too!*
>
> .   .   .   .
>
> The smiling angel dropped his pen,—
> "Why, this will never do;
> The man would be a boy again,
> And be a father too!"

"Mare Rubrum" (for 1858) was named for "the blood-red wine" praised in the first and last stanzas, but it was less a drinking song than a complex web of pastoral and biblical allusions and of concrete details held firmly in a rhythmic pattern of an octosyllabic eight-line stanza with alternate rhymes. The song for 1859 was different: "The Boys" has often been anthologized as an example of Holmes's rollicking meter and familiar fun as well as his parochial limitations. It has helped perpetuate the public image he was creating, consciously and unconsciously, but its comic poise gains value in the face of the political and social feelings that were raging furiously that year. After cutting down eight high-sounding titles to the size of boys with familiar phrases like "It's a neat little fiction,—of course it's all fudge," he gave an entire stanza to the "nice youngster of excellent pith,— / Fate tried to conceal him by naming him Smith." Samuel F. Smith was author of the popular national hymn "My country, 'tis of thee."

This Baptist preacher, whom Holmes thought he might have converted to the liberal doctrines of Unitarianism in the 1890's if he had not been so deaf, had not been sufficiently honored by his Alma Mater—of this Holmes was convinced. On March 5,1893, he wrote President Eliot to suggest that Harvard might adopt the honorary degree of Doctor of Letters, a degree given by Cambridge University in England, and that Smith would be the ideal recipient. "It will look ill on the Quinquennial of 2500 A.D. to find his name without an honorary title from his Alma Mater. . . . His song will be sung centuries from now, when most of us and our pipings are forgotten." After an apparently discouraging reply from Eliot noting that the tune accounted for the popularity of the song more than Smith's words, Holmes wrote again on March 19. He went through lines of the hymn to show that "it rises from intense personal feeling to the larger and grander sense of union in reverence of the 'Author of Liberty.'" He noted that at least an A.M., which "amounts to nothing," would be " a pleasant and a popular thing—if that is worth considering—" to give "to the little humble Baptist minister and Professor who has put a song into the mouths of the whole nation." Like Samuel Johnson, whose life, through Boswell, Holmes indulged himself in tracing through the eighteenth century as parallel to his own in the nineteenth (Johnson's being born in 1709, and himself in 1809, gave him his starting-point), Holmes valued the judgment of the general public: "a hymn that reaches the heart and expresses the feelings of millions must have a merit of its own . . .

it is the only National hymn which has gained a lodgment in the hearts of our millions. . . ."[24] But in his eighty-fourth year Holmes was really "The Last Leaf" at Harvard, and Smith never received any honorary degree from his alma mater.

Before the class meeting on January 3, 1861, South Carolina and other Southern states had seceded from the Union, and "A Voice of the Loyal North" (120) was the first of three patriotic songs Holmes wrote that year. But he brought to the class meeting a letter from Isaac Morse of New Orleans, to read aloud his regrets that he would now be separated from them by more than distance. Holmes was writing at white heat against the treason to the Union, but in April he could reply to Morse that he, too, hoped they might once again meet as loyal friends. The next poem Holmes wrote on the crisis was "Brother Jonathan's Lament for Sister Caroline" (111-12); dated March 25, 1861, it was printed, unsigned, in the *Atlantic Monthly* for May, 1861. If any reader had not identified the author of the rapid, rhythmic lines, with their turning from deep sorrow for this "child of the sun" who had "left us in passion and pride" to faith in an organic Union "of river, lake, ocean, and sky" and hope of welcoming back "our rash sister," he could do so when Holmes's volume *Songs in Many Keys* appeared in November, 1861, carrying this as the closing poem. The next month the *Atlantic* printed the "Army Hymn" (196) he had written for a patriotic gathering in May. Usually sung to the tune of "Old Hundred," it was a favorite at patriotic rallies during 1861 and 1862.

More characteristic of Holmes than the puritanical denunciation or the ringing call to arms was the ridicule effectively worked out by absurd detail and comic diction in "The Sweet Little Man / Dedicated to the Stay-at-Home Rangers" (197-98), which appeared, unsigned, in the *Transcript* for September 14, 1861. "Sweet little man" ended each stanza, and "the Apron-String Guards on the Common" in contrast to "the brave boys . . . pressing to march in the van" reached a climax in the last stanza:

> Now then, nine cheers for the Stay-at-Home Ranger!
> Blow the great fish-horn and beat the big pan!
> First in the field that is farthest from danger,
> Take your white-feather plume, sweet little man!

The change from the orator who criticized the abolitionists to the writer responding sincerely to the horror of secession and the moral call of war was not illogical: the central cause for Holmes was always the preservation of the Union, and he opposed any sentiment or action that threatened it. He had become personally involved in the fighting in April, 1861, because Oliver Wendell Holmes, Jr., had left Harvard before the completion of his senior year to enlist. Some of his classmates returned to take the examinations as requested by the faculty, but young Holmes was too busy qualifying as a lieutenant before he left for active service. He had been elected Class Poet, as his father had been, and that duty he fulfilled; he was granted his degree at commencement on July 17, 1861. His father protested to President Felton that his son was graduated without the honor due him as having been always among the top twenty in his class, but the tall son was probably already as unwilling as his mother to play any part in the witty, articulate doctor's public image—and less successful than she in keeping himself out of it. The article "Bread and the Newspaper" (the title's debt to the Roman "bread and circuses" Holmes noted in the opening lines) appeared in the *Atlantic* in September, and it reflected vividly the tensions of the Holmes family waiting for each piece of news from the front. The tone, first intimate and familiar, became serious as the author welcomed even sorrow and shame that might bring wisdom and virtue to them all. He hailed especially the feeling of unity, the comradeship that war engendered in men, whether they came from Maine or Minnesota. Especially did he welcome the disappearance of dogma before the faith and trust of sincere Christians (VIII, [1] -15).

Young Wendell was first wounded at Ball's Bluff on October 21, 1861, and his father traveled to Philadelphia, where Dr. William Hunt had given his son special care, to bring him home. He was back at the front and made a captain on March 23, 1862. In September 17, 1862, he received his second wound, at Antietam, and his father not only traveled again to find him and bring him home, but he published in the *Atlantic* for December "My Hunt After 'The Captain.'" The narrative, still exciting, begins with the message at night: "wound shot through the neck though not mortal." The accurate details of conditions Holmes met on his journey to the battle zone are still informative, especially for what they reveal of the lack of organization and communication, or of the special favors granted a well-known author, such as a "sight-seeing" trip to Antietam when mule-teams with supplies were crowding the roads. The sentiment at the end, "our boys learn that life is noble only when it is held cheap by the side of honor and duty" (VIII, 77), was in sharp contrast to war seen as "organized barbarism," which both father and son were later to call it.

The Class Poem for 1862 was another on the current crisis, "Voyage of the Good Ship Union" (120-21). The conventional figure was sharpened by references to places as the ship voyaged south, from "the Pilgrim's Cape" and "Manhattan's narrowing bay," where all was safe, to the gathering mists off Delaware and Fort Monroe and the flames and shadows over Beaufort and Sumter. Among the many war poems Holmes wrote in response to specific demands during 1862-63, three revealed him stirred to the Puritan wrath he had often decried; Puritan also was his turning to the Bible for title and imagery. " 'Thus Saith the Lord, I Offer Thee Three Things' " was a recruiting poem for Ward Six in Boston, after that ward had failed to provide its quota of soldiers. Ward Six included Charles Street, and the Holmes family had moved to No. 21 in July, 1858, when business had come uncomfortably close to the house in Montgomery Place. Charles Street was pleasantly residential, with the Charles River in sight and the Fields's home almost next door. But business soon drove Holmes out of this house too (the number had been changed to 164 in 1866), and he moved to a new house at 296 Beacon Street in November, 1870, which remained in the family for seventy years. But in August, 1862, Holmes was the natural one on Charles Street to turn to for a rhythmic call to duty, and he responded in ringing tones, offering three things: "to go, to wait, to stay" and, if the last, "Dead to their country's woe and shame."

" 'Choose Ye This Day Whom Ye Will Serve' " was written for the Reverend Thomas Starr King to read at the close of a lecture on Holmes he was to give in San Francisco in December, 1862. King had asked for a poem because he was afraid California was slipping back into its earlier pro-Southern feeling. When Holmes read this poem at the Class Meeting January 8, 1863, the choice he offered between "the proud planter" whose voice was "lost in the shriek of his victim's despair" and "the Puritan's prayer . . . strangle the monster that struggles to birth" was more appropriate for a wavering audience in San Francisco than for the Boys of '29. "To Canaan," subtitled "A Puritan War Song," appeared in the Boston *Transcript* for August 12, 1862. Two days later it was sung at a recruiting meeting in Salem. Again names and diction echoed Old Testament strife and battle for truth: "break the tyrant's sceptre" and "build the people's throne."

The close of the "Three Things" poem of August, 1862, was "answer NOW," the last word echoing from a call to arms he had sounded in July at the Harvard Phi Beta Kappa dinner, "Now Or Never" (changed for publication to "Never Or Now: An Appeal," 192-93). "Never Or Now" began two stanzas and four lines and ended the poem, summoning "young heroes" to be true and to fight for their heritage of freedom.

The desperate need for strength and endurance expressed in these poems was echoed in the oration Holmes gave for the city of Boston on July 4, 1863. Later entitled "The Inevitable Trial" (VIII [77]-120), the speech directly attacked "the living question of the hour" and pointed out that every month made the cause the North defended more crucial and the need for united action more pressing. "Not to have fought would have been to be false to liberty everywhere, and to humanity." The reformers he had been so temperamentally averse to, he defended here: "They may be unwise, violent, abusive, extravagant, impracticable, but they are alive at any rate, and it is their business to remove abuses as soon as they are dead, and often to help them to die." He also reversed his attitude of gentle ridicule of patriotic orations and their full-blown sentiments: "In all questions involving duty, we act from sentiments." But he offered close reasoning more than sentiments: the conflict had come as a result of a long-growing difference between the states of North and South, and maintaining the Union would now cost a high price; "it will not hurt our people to be taught that there are other things to be cared for besides money-making and money-spending. . . . War is a grim business," and devours money paid in taxes as well as blood. Only in the last paragraph, addressed to the "Citizens of Boston," did he exhort to united action and support with time-worn phrases like "wounds of living heroes," "graves of fallen martyrs," and "the hopes of your children." The subject was so timely and the presentation so vigorous and persuasive that many printings were made in Boston; a patriot in Philadelphia had it printed and distributed free there.

After this success, the lecture-poisoning again took hold of Holmes, and he delivered "The Weaning of Young America" at

Tremont Temple, Boston, on November 3, 1863, and in Brooklyn on November 6. Sharp words against England characterized this speech. The country the child Wendell had become aware of as our enemy in two wars had not won his devotion as France had when he studied and traveled abroad from 1833 to 1835, and now England's support of the South had made her appear even more "a nation of shopkeepers" to him. But he recognized this speech as of contemporary use only, and it was never published among his collected works. Another lecture, "New England's Master-Key," first given in Cambridge on November 15, 1864, was concerned less with the national crisis than with the demanding heritage of his own region.[25]

The Class Poem for 1864 had been on the war, but it indicated a more hopeful mood—"The Last Charge" (123-24). Men of the North were still summoned to the conflict, but "The dog-star of treason grows dim in the sky." In 1865, "Sherman's in Savannah" (124-25) was a rhythmic shout of joy, with "Savannah" effectively used at the close of each stanza. Now Holmes's mood was relaxed enough to permit another poem, "Our Oldest Friend" (124), in the familiar, playful tone of earlier days.

> So here's a health in homely rhyme
> To our oldest classmate, Father Time!
> May our last survivor live to be
> As bald and as wise and as tough as he!

In 1865, two other occasions had demanded his songs: on June 1, Memorial Services for President Lincoln in Boston; on July 21, Commemoration Services at Harvard. A lecture "Poetry of the War" was given by Holmes in New York,[26] and repeated often in and around Boston. He chose Lowell as the first poet, probably because the latter's noble "Commemoration Ode" was still ringing in his fellow-poet's ears. Holmes used his own Puritan War Song, published anonymously in 1862, which he noted had been claimed by three authors (191); he must have decided "To Canaan" was worth claiming for himself, even if—or because—it did sound like the early Puritans.

These were by no means the only occasional poems Holmes was asked for and wrote during these years, but they offer a fair sampling. In 1866, the Class Poem "My Annual" returned to sentiments of warm and proved affection, noting only that peace had come at last. His personal affection, unaltered by the war, was expressed in a memorial notice for the New Orleans classmate Isaac Morse, who died in February, which ended with the lines: "The blazon of Union spreads full in the sun; / We echo its words,—We are one! We are one!" This memorial notice was sent to the Morse family, and the friendship the classmates had hoped to take up again unchanged was kept up by affectionate exchanges through the years between Holmes and Morse's son and daughter.

The titles of the Class Poems for 1867 and 1868, "All Here" and "Once More," indicate their mood and theme. The year 1869 called forth two Class Poems, "The Old Cruiser" (128-29) and a hymn (129-30). The vivid analogy of "The Old Cruiser" gave it sparkle enough to be used also at the Harvard Alumni Meeting on June 29, but Holmes added four stanzas. The number aboard was now down to thirty, but the jester's mixture of joy and loss was as easy in this poem as in "Bill and Joe":

> In thirty goblets the wine was poured,
> But threescore gathered around the board,—
> For lo! at the side of every chair
> A shadow hovered—we all were there!

The hymn "Thou Gracious Power, whose mercy lends / The light of home, the smile of friends" was tender, brief, and melodious; it has continued to be sung at fraternal and religious gatherings which have continuity.

In 1870, besides the Class Poem, he gave verses at the laying of the cornerstone of Memorial Hall in Cambridge on October 6; these were poignant with the heavy loss of young lives of promise. Loss had not touched him so closely as it had Lowell, with four nephews slain, but young Wendell had been wounded three times, and too many of his comrades did not return. The lines beginning "Not with the anguish of hearts that are breaking" (214) conveyed sensitively a memory yet green though "Hushed are their battle-fields, ended their marches." In contrast, his lines for the dedication of Memorial Hall on June 23, 1874, were perfunctory with the trite figures of "Mother" and "marble pages" (215). Often for the class meetings in these years he gave verses in memory of those who had died, with initials only as titles. But in 1874, figure and play returned with "Our

Banker" (135-36), none other than "Old Time," who was offered a health at the end as "the wrinkled old miser, our friend; / May he send us his bills till the century's end."[27]

In the Class Poem for 1877, "How Not To Settle It" (138-39), Holmes returned to national politics; the Presidential election had not been settled in November, 1876, but had become a bitter, threatening contest until March 2, 1877, when Republican Hayes was announced as victor over the Democratic Tilden. Grant's reliance on the military and the scandals of his administration had left a country ready to start another Civil War, this time on party lines. Holmes made the passions involved ridiculous by devices like the feminine rhyme—*filled in* to rhyme with *Tilden*—and by suggesting that his Class fight it out. He emphasized "those civilians" to satirize the reliance on the military and the "Bloody Shirt":

> I say once more, as I have said before,
> If voting for our Tildens and our Hayeses
> Means only fight, then, Liberty, good night!
> Pack up your ballot-box and go to blazes!

A special value is attached to Holmes's comic poise at this juncture, for personal financial worries were harrying him. The old gambrel-roofed house in Cambridge had been sold to Harvard, and the $55,000 had been invested in Western Railway stock under the guidance of a Harvard benefactor who had made his fortune by such speculation. When it appeared that the whole sum had been lost, with no steady income resulting for sister Ann Upham in Salem, brother John in Cambridge, and Wendell in Boston, Holmes was frantic—and as baffled by the economic situation in 1877 as he had been by the political climate in 1855. But he could rattle off his jest for the Boys "who will all love it because it is mine."

By exaggeration and rollicking rhymes, a national situation potentially shocking was made to invite the intellectual approach of comedy instead of the passionate partisanship which had seized the country. That Holmes was satisfied with the result of the election, and not so troubled about its honesty as historians have been since, was emphasized in his poem "To Rutherford Birchard Hayes" (239), which he read "At the Dinner to the President, Boston, June 26, 1877." He hailed him as "His Honesty, the President" and "Healer of Strife." At the Woodstock festivities on July 4, 1877, where "A Family Record" renewed tender memories of his father and his father's ancestors, his "Sentiment" was a brief "Ship of State" (239), which recalled that "the ship came too near wreck, / In the long quarrel for the quarter-deck," and invoked God to "guide the honest hand that holds her wheel"—"honest" once more made emphatic.

In 1878, the Harvard verses Holmes wrote which received the most attention were two sonnets he sent to the Harvard Club of New York at the request of its president, his old friend and editor John O. Sargent. In "Two Sonnets: Harvard" (251), Holmes contrasted the motto "Christo et Ecclesiae" of 1700, with the older "Veritas" of 1643. As scientist and liberal religious thinker—almost at times crusader—Holmes preferred "the white hand" of "brave truth" to the "narrow door" of "godly zealots." A surprising number of Harvard alumni who were obviously alarmed at "modern heresies" protested his choice, even carrying the controversy to the president and the Board of Overseers lest they be persuaded by this Harvard spokesman to change the 1700 motto on the Harvard seal. Holmes's letter which accompanied the sonnets showed him chiefly interested in the sonnet form, as he had written of poetic form to Lowell and Emerson earlier: "A slow minuet of rhythms stepping in measured cadences over a mosaic pavement of rhyme, and which not rarely combines a minimum of thought with a maximum of labor."[28]

The Class Poem for 1879, "The Archbishop and Gil Blas: A Modernized Version" (141-42), went back in its allusive title to the years in Paris; but it was made humorously immediate and vivid by the dialogue which found the stubborn old man forced to admit his sight and hearing might be failing, but "I'm hale and brisk and sound." But more prominent in 1879 than this play on old age in the Class Poem was the one he wrote for a social and literary celebration of which he was the center. On December 3 the publishers of the *Atlantic Monthly* gave a "Breakfast" at the Brunswick Hotel to which prominent figures were invited to bring or send tributes in honor of Holmes's seventieth birthday (August 29). "The Iron Gate" (243-44) again showed Holmes easily combining the classical image of the title with the diction of Christian faith. Though the poem mentioned "curfew" and ended with "farewell," it was not sad.

"I, who have never deemed it sin to gladden / This vale of shadows with a wholesome laugh" named a public image people recognized with warm pleasure. The "iron portal" might shut off a life which was neglecting the patriarch, but gates of pearl were showing "in the glimmering starlight." *The Iron Gate* was part of the title of the book of his poems published in 1880.[29] The *Other Poems* of the title were chiefly occasional: a memorial "To James Freeman Clarke / April 4, 1880" (255) articulated a deep personal loss; his fiftieth anniversary as a Harvard alumnus was celebrated in "Vestigia Quinque Retrorsum" (244-47), which he read at the commencement dinner on June 25, 1879. "The School-Boy" (257-62) had been read at the centennial celebration of the founding of Phillips Academy, Andover. The Academy did not soon forget this student of one year: in 1909, the centennial of his birth was celebrated; in 1929, the new library was dedicated as the Oliver Wendell Holmes Memorial Library.

By 1880 "The Shadows" (142-43) had really begun to take over, as the number of the Class of '29 physically present had dropped below twenty. In that year Holmes was awarded the honorary degree of Doctor of Laws by Harvard. But three degrees from Harvard—in 1829, in 1836, and in 1880—proved to be not sufficient for Holmes; in December, 1888, he was living enough in the past to decide he would like to have the A.M. his class had rebelled against getting for a few extra dollars. His letter to President Eliot reveals how his fondness for all Harvard associations increased with the years.

Circumstances have called my attention to the fact that I have never received my degree of A.M. from my Alma Mater. Many of my Class declined to take it, I among the rest. I am unhappy without it—it looks as if my Alma Mater didn't love me. The degree used to cost fifteen dollars—perhaps you would sell me one for that price or give it to me—*honoris causa* or for other sufficient reason—chiefly because I want it. I cannot afford to go down to posterity on the immortal *Catalogues* as having despised any honor of the University, or being thought unworthy of so humble a one as a A.M.[30]

Needless to say, the old man's whim was gratified; he was awarded an A.M. *honoris causa* at commencement in 1889.

The poem of 1887, "The Broken Circle" (147), revealed analogy as still strong in the aging poet and this annual rite of singing to and for his classmates as pervading his experiences no matter how far removed in space or circumstance. In 1886, during his English visit, he had revisited Stonehenge, a scene which had made a deep impression on the young medical student of 1834. But his memory of fifty years seemed a trifle at Stonehenge: "Nothing dwarfs an individual life like one of these massive, almost unchanging monuments of an antiquity which refuses to be measured" (X, 110-11). The individual class poet did take over, however, and Holmes dropped into the middle of his English travels the account of reading the poem he wrote about this "broken circle of stones" to the eight out of the original fifty-nine who were able to gather in January, 1887, to hear their plight, the "wrecks of friendship's broken ring," pictured on "Sarum's treeless plain"—but with the difference that their altar-fire was still burning, not cold and gray like the "Druid stones."

The last Class Poem, "After the Curfew" (148) in 1889, carried the word *curfew* from "The Iron Gate" of 1879, through the last volume of poems *Before the Curfew* of 1888, to "After" of the next year. Since this poem used the figure of a play on the stage and ended "I let the curtain fall," Holmes was mocking his resemblance to the player who specialized in "farewell" appearances. Phrases and mood recalled "The Old Player" of 1855, when the man, not yet fifty, imagined "a play of seventy years"—ten fewer than when he next announced the "play" was over.

In 1890, the surviving members—Gray, May, Smith, and Storrow—dined with Holmes at 296 Beacon Street with no mention of a song. The last meeting of the Class of '29 was on May 31, 1893, when four of the five living members—Holmes, May, Smith, and Storrow—dined at 296 Beacon Street, and then went to the Young Men's Christian Union to hear Holmes read his next-to-last occasional poem, "Hymn Written for the Twenty-Fifth Anniversary of the Reorganization of the Boston Young Men's Christian Union" (298). The religious position stated was Holmes's characteristic rejection of a creed of wrath and his stress on faith and love:

Our Father! while our hearts unlearn
The creeds that wrong thy name,
Still let our hallowed altars burn
With faith's undying flame!

Not by the lightning-gleams of wrath
Our souls thy face shall see,
The star of Love must light the path
That leads to Heaven and Thee.

Holmes's last occasional poem was read at a special meeting
of the Massachusetts Historical Society on November 21, 1893,
in memory of Francis Parkman (298-99). He celebrated the
"later craftsman," who like Prescott and Motley "wove their
pictured webs in History's loom." The last two stanzas were
reprinted in October, 1894, as being appropriate for Holmes
himself:

Halting with feeble steps, or bending o'er
The sweet-breathed roses which he loved so well,
While through long years his burdening cross he bore,
From those firm lips no coward accents fell.

A brave, bright memory! his the stainless shield
No shame defaces and no envy mars!
When our far future's record is unsealed
His name will shine among its morning stars.

Though Holmes had borne no such burden of ill-health as
Parkman had carried, the years after his wife's and daughter's
deaths in 1888 and 1889 had been lonely, and he had clung
more tenaciously than ever to the precious associations of his
class, and to the role of occasional poet which kept him young.
May recorded the last official act of the Class of 1829 in the
Class Book: he and Smith attended the funeral of Holmes at
King's Chapel at noon on October 10, 1894.

I have followed the thread of the Harvard Class Poems, with
other Harvard connections and the brief but memorable ex-
cursions into contemporary subjects at times of crisis, to carry
through Holmes's career as poet and topical writer, before
taking up the major contributions he made to American literature as a writer of prose essay and fiction. But the poet can
never be excluded. Following a straight line in discussing Holmes

as man and as author is made difficult by the competent, often distinguished verse or prose he could produce on any subject which caught his interest momentarily, and which the many sections of society he was actively a part of were constantly asking him for. Therefore occasional writings keep weaving in and out of his more classifiable forms and subjects, and I shall take them up further as they have become significant of themselves or as they illuminate his literary career. The range and success of his public performances are important for any fair evaluation as well as for understanding the wide fame Holmes enjoyed during the nineteenth century in the United States and in England.

CHAPTER 3

The Breakfast-Table Series

IN DECEMBER, 1884, when Holmes was opening the "New Portfolio" with his third and last novel *A Mortal Antipathy*, he devoted the first number to an introduction in which he talked over with "the whole family of readers belonging to my list of intimates" (VII [1]-32) his career as a man of letters up to that time. His first Portfolio began with the poems for occasions and for the "showy annuals," but its contents had "boyhood written on every page." The "best scraps" he justly selected from the first Portfolio were "Old Ironsides . . . a single passionate outcry when the old war-ship I had read about . . . was threatened with demolition"; and "The Last Leaf" suggested by old Major Melville in his cocked hat and breeches. The second Portfolio was opened in the autumn of 1857, when the *Atlantic Monthly* "which I had the honor of naming was started by the enterprising firm of Phillips & Sampson, under the editorship of Mr. James Russell Lowell."

After the success of the magazine was assured, Holmes and Lowell each generously cited the part the other had played in that achievement. It cannot now be accurately measured how much urging Holmes needed to set down in print the kind of talk which had made him sought after as companion and speaker at gatherings formal and informal. Whether coincidental or causative, Lowell as editor and Holmes as the writer of an easy, concrete prose neatly alternating with poems that gave emphasis or variety, helped to make successful the first literary magazine in this country to have an enduring life. The *Atlantic* could take advantage of many talents: the melody of Longfellow; the lyric intensity of Whittier; the fascinating thought and expression of Emerson; the haunting power of Hawthorne, "the great Romancer"; and the vivid exposition of the scientist Agassiz and the diplomat Motley. Besides all these, to balance the more radical reformers like Underwood and Lowell who had cut their editorial teeth on abolitionist papers, Holmes's record indicated he could be counted upon for brief and witty comment; if he did ridicule, surprise and recognition removed the sting.

I   *The Autocrat*

When Holmes wrote the opening number of *The Autocrat of the Breakfast-Table,* as Autocrat he took up the advantages of Societies of Mutual Admiration, with "the young man named John" and the divinity student dissenting. He cited as an example the *Société de l'Observation Médicale* to which he had belonged in Paris, and an American club of which he was not a member but which thrived on the well-deserved admiration exchanged among the generous company of "artists, authors, philanthropists, men of science." That he was not a member of the Saturday Club until October 31, before the first number of the *Atlantic* appeared in November, 1857, was probably because, with other studies and duties, he was "outside of the charmed circle drawn around the scholars and poets of Cambridge and Concord" (VII, 10). The club met the last Saturday of each month at the Parker House in Boston.

At his class dinners Holmes had come to take it for granted that he would play an important part, by warm loyalty, by quick repartee, and by reading at least one poem. Although many of "The Boys" were wealthier or of higher social background than he, his place was secure. But the Saturday Club was a place of exchange rather than performance; and although both Lowell and Holmes inclined to take over as if on the lecture platform, such self-indulgence came later rather than at the beginning of his membership, when Holmes was gratified to be accepted in the group headed by Longfellow and Agassiz and including Emerson and Hawthorne, the lawyers Rockwood Hoar and Richard Henry Dana, and the society leaders Sam Ward and Tom Appleton. The anecdote which tells of the meeting of the club after the *Atlantic* had just come out when each member sat down quietly to read his own contribution is probably not a gross exaggeration. That both Lowell and Holmes were quick of wit and word and enjoyed a verbal fencing-match gives substance to the story that when the Saturday Club entertained the Reverend Calvin Stowe and his wife Harriet Beecher, at one end of the table Lowell was busy proving to the daughter of the crusading Beechers and the author of *Uncle Tom's Cabin* that Fielding's lusty *Tom Jones* was the greatest novel ever written while at the other end Holmes was explaining to the Reverend Calvin Stowe that people learned their swearing from ministers in the pulpit.

The Saturday Club and the *Atlantic Monthly* were two important outlets for Holmes which also enriched his life. The people concerned with the new magazine were frankly amazed at the immediate popularity of *The Autocrat of the Breakfast-Table*. The title and pattern depended on the dramatic scene Holmes had first created twenty-five years earlier; the Autocrat was now more experienced and assured and the other figures more sharply etched, often more recognizable as types, like "the economically organized female in the black bombazine." Holmes remarked it was "dipped from the running stream of my thoughts." An important key to its success was that it answered so well the second reason Holmes gave as justification for an author: the first was if he had a story to tell that everyone wanted to hear; the second, "if he can put in fitting words any common experiences not already well told, so that readers will say, 'Why, yes! I have had that sensation, thought, emotion, a hundred times, but I never heard it spoken of before, and I never saw any mention of it in print'" (I, 12).

The pleasure readers still derive from the books of the Breakfast-Table series is that of recognition, with a subsequent quickening of interest to find out what the author has made of the human interplay he has developed. The richness Holmes offered in his treatment was only rarely of philosophical depth or lyrical intensity, but frequent analogies with concrete vividness threw light on some aspect of a situation we all recognize. Thus Truth was contrasted with "an old lying falsehood" in the shape of a flat stone that kills normal growth and breeds "hideous crawling creatures" which come to light when the stone is turned over by one who "puts the staff of truth to the old lying incubus"; children are early given a choice between the cubes of truth which won't roll, have "a great talent for standing still, and always keep right side up" and the spheres of lies "which are the most convenient things in the world" because they roll so easily, but "are apt to roll into the wrong corner, and to get out of his way when he most wants them" (I, 111-16). Sprinkled among these concrete images which suggest more than they say are brief quotable statements: "Good feeling helps society to make liars of most of us,—not absolute liars, but such careless handlers of truth that its sharp corners get terribly rounded"; or, at the opening of the next number, "Sin has many tools, but a lie is the handle which fits them all."

Familiar diction gives an extra tang to comments like "All lecturers, all professors, all schoolmasters, have ruts and grooves into which their conversation is perpetually sliding" (I, 65): "habit is a labor-saving invention which enables a man to get along with less fuel" (I, 155); "They [cant or slang terms instead of precise words] are the blank checks of intellectual bankruptcy;—you may fill them up with what idea you like; it makes no difference, for there are no funds in the treasury upon which they are drawn" (I, 256). Figures contributed to the sharp effects, and were quick and suggested in a word or two or followed through with growing relevance, as in his picture of human feelings:

> Every person's feelings have a front-door and a side-door by which they must be entered. The front-door is on the street. . . . This front-door leads into a passage which opens into an anteroom, and this into the interior apartments. The side-door opens at once into the sacred chambers. . . .
>
> Be very careful to whom you trust one of these keys of the side-door. The fact of possessing one renders those even who are dear to you very terrible at times. You can keep the world from your front-door, or receive visitors only when you are ready for them; but those of your own flesh and blood, or of certain grades of intimacy, can come in at the side-door, if they will, at any hour or in any mood. . . .
>
> No stranger can get a great many notes of torture out of a human soul; it takes one that knows it well,—parent, child, brother, sister, intimate. Be very careful to whom you give a side-door key; too many have them already (I, 128-30).

Dramatic interplay gives variety, and makes extreme statements acceptable or ridiculous. The landlady is primarily concerned with keeping her boarders; her son Benjamin Franklin proves convenient for errands, for interruptions, for instruction in French and Latin. The Poor Relation provides an acid touch, but the most effective dissenter is the young fellow named John, who has both feet on the ground as well as active voice and hands. When the Autocrat has outlined psychologically the six personalities taking part in a dialogue between John and Thomas—"I. The real John; known only to his Maker. / 2. John's ideal John; never the real one, and often very unlike him. / 3. Thomas's ideal John; never the real John, nor John's John, but often very unlike either" and three similar Thomases (I, 53)—the literal John took the remaining peaches in the basket before it reached the Autocrat, since "there was just one apiece for him." The divinity student and the old gentleman opposite speak up less frequently; the former is the voice of dogma, the latter is wise in years and experience. The school-mistress is a contrast to the landlady's daughter in appearance, taste, and manner, and she provides the romantic finale as she and the Autocrat take "the long path together." The Autocrat hints that the romance comes at the request of his readers: they, especially the women, were as advisory as to what should happen in the next number as Richardson's had been about what should happen to Pamela and Clarissa Harlowe. It was Holmes's fault; he admitted, "I purr very loud over a good honest letter that says pretty things to me" (I, 289).

Holmes often uses his intimacy with his readers to give them advice: although he is not so didactic as the modern *How To Read A Book* (he would surely have preferred *How To Read Two Books*), he asks that his readers be creative; that they realize the "saturation-point of each mind differs" (I, 133); that the reader's imagination is needed to transfigure "a string of trivialities" (I, 199). Holmes states a preference for life over books that recalls Emerson's *American Scholar* which he had heard at Harvard in 1837. After distinguishing between the use and abuse of books, Emerson asserted: "Books are for the scholar's idle times. When he can read God directly, the hour is too precious to be wasted in other men's transcripts of their readings." Holmes accents the mind: "there are times in which every active mind feels itself above any and all human books"; or he asserts: "I always believed in life rather than in books" (I, 132, 134). Like Dr. Johnson too in finding books no substitute for life, Holmes announced the game he was playing with the eighteenth-century *magister* by his subtitle here: "Every Man His Own Boswell." The most detailed account of the game of identity Holmes gave on December 13, 1884, when "I have just lost my dear and honored contemporary of the last century." Since Johnson was baptized on the day he was born and Holmes not for three weeks, the date, September 18, was the same in 1709 and 1809. "Year by year, and almost month by month, my life has kept pace in this century with his life in the last century. . . . It was for me a kind of unison between two instruments, both playing that old familiar air, 'Life,'—one a bassoon, if you will, and the other an oaten pipe" (VII, 20-21).

The Autocrat has to share the stage with two facets of Holmes's career already established—the Poet and the Professor: ". . . I think myself fortunate in having the Poet and the Professor for my intimates. We are so much together, that we no doubt think and talk a good deal alike; yet our points of view are in many respects individual and peculiar" (I, 178-79). The Poet offers only one poem, the occasional "A Good Time Going" (I, 223-24; 155-56), which Holmes had written for a farewell dinner for Charles Mackay on May 18, 1858. The preface to the poem in the *Autocrat* explains how eager the Poet is to leave town before the anniversaries begin and he will have to "get up and make speeches, or songs, or toasts." Like the poem, the protest here is perfunctory and lifeless compared to the fireworks of the Autocrat's talk or the vivacity Holmes could muster on this subject in a letter to T. W. Higginson on September 30, 1872, after he had been succumbing to such demands for another ten years.

> Your kind words are pleasant and your request is far from un-reasonable, yet I must excuse myself from the very slight task—as it seems at least—to which you invite me.
>
> I am thoroughly tired of my own voice at all sorts of occasional gatherings. I have handled the epithets of eulogy until the mere touch of a warm adjective blisters my palm. I have tried not to do myself discredit by unseemly flattery, but I do really feel as if by force of repetition my welcomes were growing if not unwelcome, at least outworn, and should in common propriety give place to something a little fresher. I have greeted representatives from all parts of the civilized and half-civilized world and am expecting to be called on whenever the King of Dahomey or a minister from Ujiji makes his appearance.
>
> The most desperate attempts were made by men with argument and women with entreaty to get me to play Orpheus to the stones of the Pittsfield monument, but I resisted both successfully. These invitations keep coming to me all the time, and I mean to decline

them all unless for some very special reason that happens to strike me full in the centre of volition. Here are Froude, and Edmund Yates, and George MacDonald, and nobody knows how many more—Tyndall and by and by perhaps Huxley and one must draw the line somewhere—suppose we say "Rhyming done here only for crowned heads or their representatives?" I have done England, France, Russia (twice), China, Japan, Germany (in the person of Ehrenberg) and so belabored my own countrymen of every degree with occasional verses that I must have coupled "name" and "fame" together scores of times and made "story" and "glory" as intimate as if they had been born twins.

I know you are on your knees by this time asking the Lord to forgive you for making a suggestion that I should try this last experiment on the patience of mankind. I cannot say whether He will forgive you or not but you have my full pardon inasmuch as you have joined a very complimentary request with a word of praise which coming from so good a judge of what will bear praising makes me willing to do almost anything except what you ask me to.[1]

This delightful play of concrete detail, exaggeration, colorful diction combined with the winning personal tone of the verbal *tour de force* at the end reveals Holmes still writing, on occasion in 1872, as he had written for *The Autocrat* in 1857-58. It is as Holmes the talker that the Autocrat shines: "Sometimes it becomes almost a physical necessity to talk out what is in the mind, before putting anything else into it" (I, 134) helps explain the social trait he was famous for. "Real talkers" are defined as "people with fresh ideas, of course, and plenty of good warm words to dress them in" (I, 143). But the Autocrat warns against wit; an author is not pleased to be told he is droll because he knows, like the clown, that the women are not in love with him but with "the fellow in the black coat and plumed hat" and that his place is "at the tail of the procession." A figure of white light in contrast to colored lights, which is one of the "grooves" into which Holmes's "conversation is perpetually sliding," illuminates his estimate of wit. A single ray of color—red, yellow, blue—illustrates that wit "consists in a partial and incomplete view of whatever it touches. . . . We get beautiful effects from wit,—all the prismatic colors,—but never the object as it is in fair daylight. . . . Poetry uses the rainbow tints for special effects, but always keeps its essential object in the purest white light of truth" (I, 50). Within a paragraph contrasting lights have led him from *wit* to *poetry*. To illustrate how easily he could slide into this "groove" and how genuinely he could fuse the truth of poetry with the truth of religion, another use of this figure in a letter to a lady who was trying to interest him in her newly adopted religion, Roman Catholicism, may be cited:

> I think myself that this planet is lighted by a stained window. One sees through a blue pane, another through a red or yellow one—but outside the light is white, and those see it most truly who are next an *open* window.
>
> But I do not quarrel with this saint because he (or she more likely) is in a patch of blue light or with that other because she is in a yellow one. The accidents of your church please my taste and stimulate my imagination. I love the pictures, the incense, the tingling of the boyish choristers' voices. There is the difference between your service and the puritan preachment that there is between the maple in October, dressed in its flaming robes, and the same tree in January naked in the blast. But the course of nature is that the painted leaves must fall, and the bare tree bud with new foliage.[2]

The Autocrat is rich in biographical intimacies of Holmes. His moving to Charles Street in 1858 had meant that the Charles River was his backyard, and he could indulge in boating, the outdoor activity he enjoyed next after riding and driving fast horses, which had become expensive and inconvenient with the Pittsfield vacations gone. The Autocrat gives a full account of the three boats Holmes owned and used on the river, especially the race-boat and the pride he took in his speed and skill rowing on the river and in the bay. Travel in Italy and the voice of a child in Paris are part of the Autocrat's memories, and he uses Holmes's Class Poem for 1854, "The Old Man Dreams." He begins a series of three figures with the class and its log of competition, the opening epigrammatic: "I find the great thing in this world is not so much where we stand, as in what direction we are moving" (I, 93). The Derby is used as the image for commencement, and the log is checked through the decades against individual achievements. The third figure is of the sea-shell, the Pearly Nautilus, and the passage closes with Holmes's poetic masterpiece "The Chambered Nautilus" (I, 97; 149-50).

The success of this poem, growing out of a close following of one idea through many pages and using as concrete image an object he had long known and studied, argues for the truth of his statement: "Certain things are good for nothing until they have been kept for a long while; and some are good for nothing until they have been kept and used. . . . Of those which must be kept and used I will name three,—meerschaum pipes, violins, and poems" (I, 101). In the poem, "The ship of pearl" is described in the first stanza and wrecked in the second with such suggestive diction as "shadowed main," "webs of living gauze," and "irised ceiling"; the stanza has a special lyric beauty, with the change to the short lines Holmes had early displayed a mastery of. The brevity, the melody, and the artful consistency of image have won it continuing praise, although the proportion of two stanzas for the exposition of the idea as against three for the concrete image is almost too much for the twentieth-century aversion to any *So live's*. But the vocabulary keeps the coils of the shell with the lesson to the end: "Leaving thine outgrown shell by life's unresting sea!"

This poem was one of the two that Osler suggested when he expressed the wish that Holmes would evaluate his own contributions to medicine and to poetry. Osler was writing of doctors who were also men of letters; and, after mentioning Goldsmith and Keats, he continued:

> The most conspicuous modern example of success in both fields is offered by the Autocrat of the Breakfast Table, who for many years occupied the Chair of Anatomy at Harvard, and who as a young man made permanent contributions to practical medicine. In his last book, "Our Hundred Days in Europe," he mentions having sat next to Mr. Lawson Tait at dinner and he suggests the question, "Which would give most satisfaction to a thoroughly humane and unselfish being of cultivated intelligence and lively sense—to have written the plays which Shakespeare has left for an inheritance to mankind, or to have snatched from the jaws of death scores of suffering women and restored them to a sound and comfortable existence?" I know of no man who could so well make answer to this question as the Autocrat himself. Would he rather go down to posterity as the man who, in this country at least, first roused the profession to a sense of the perils of puerperal fever as an infectious disease—and who thereby has probably saved more lives than Lawson Tait—and whose essay on the subject—*pace*

shades of Meigs and Hodge—is a classic in American literature, or would he choose to be remembered as the author of "The Pearly Nautilus" and "The Last Leaf"?

The printed query came to Holmes's attention, and in his reply to Osler he chose to consider only "The Chambered Nautilus" as the poem.

I have rarely been more pleased than by your allusions to an old paper of mine. There was a time certainly in which I would have said that the best page of my record was that in which I had fought my battle for the poor poisoned women. I am reminded of that essay from time to time, but it was published in a periodical which died after one year's life, and therefore escaped the wider notice it would have found if printed in the American Journal of Medical Sciences. A lecturer at one of the great London hospitals referred to it the other day and coupled it with some fine phrases about myself which made me blush, either with modesty or vanity, I forget which.

I think I will not answer the question you put me. I think oftenest of "The Chambered Nautilus," which is a favorite poem of mine, though I wrote it myself. The essay only comes up at long intervals, the poem repeats itself in my memory. And is very often spoken of by correspondents in terms of more than ordinary praise. I had a savage pleasure, I confess, in handling those two Professors —learned men both of them, skillful experts, but babies, as it seemed to me, in their capacity of reasoning and arguing. But in writing the poem I was filled with a better feeling, the highest state of mental exaltation and the most crystalline clairvoyance, as it seemed to me, that had ever been granted to me—I mean that lucid vision of one's thought and all forms of expression which will be at once precise and musical, which is the poet's special gift, however large or small in amount or value. There is more selfish pleasure to be had out of the poem—perhaps a nobler satisfaction from the life-saving labor.[3]

Once again Holmes reveals that he held firm ideas about a poet's experience and expression.

Of the poems the Autocrat gave as his own, the most sentimental and the one which drew the most popular response, especially from women, was "The Voiceless" (I, 306-7; 99). It appeared in the parenthesis "The Long Path" which the Autocrat was taking with the schoolmistress, and it was addressed to

"hearts that break and give no sign." The last four lines of the
stanza were the ones most often requested by autograph collectors or for sale at the many charitable fairs during and
after the Civil War. To such charities Holmes sometimes sent
as many as a hundred signed autograph copies of specified lines.

> A few can touch the magic string,
> And noisy Fame is proud to win them;—
> Alas for those who never sing,
> And die with all their music in them!

The humorous play the Autocrat often indulged in is illustrated by two of the poems he recited for the group at the
Breakfast-Table. One was later given the title "Ode for a
Social Meeting / With slight alterations by a teetotaler" (I, 48;
162), and it shows Holmes completely recovered from any
restraint Lowell's objections might have suggested: in the line
". . . summer's last roses lie hid in the wines," *last roses* is crossed
out and *rank poisons* written in, and the last line is altered
from "Long live the gay servant that laughs for us all" to
"Down, down with the tyrant that masters us all." The poem
"Contentment" with the epigraph "Man wants but little here
below" (I, 268-70; 157-58) reveals a more subtly developed
irony than this exercise, and it shows the Autocrat—and Holmes—
laughing at the importance both give to ancestors, a library and
family portraits, and tasteful elegance. "Simple tastes" are defined as content with "Titians and Raphaels three or four," *one*
Stradivarius but *two* Meerschaums, "A ruby and a pearl or so":

> Wealth's wasteful tricks I will not learn,
> Nor ape the glittering upstart fool;—
>
> .   .   .   .
>
> Thus humble let me live and die,
> Nor long for Midas' golden touch,
> If Heaven more generous gifts deny,
> I shall not miss them *much*,—
>
> .   .   .   .

In *The Autocrat* Holmes saved some of his reminiscences and
characteristic verses for the Professor; like Holmes, he had
resided at Central Court, at Dartmouth, and along the Housa-
tonic. Literary allusions were divided between the Professor and

the Autocrat: the latter spoke tenderly of Cowper's poem about his mother's picture and composed a Houyhnhnm Gazette in which his horses won Swift's Gulliver by offering lilac leaves and hyacinths till his "eyes filled as if with raindrops"; the Professor turned Cicero's "De Senectute" into journalistic English remarks on old age, revising some Latin phrases to match the familiar English. He shared Holmes's preference for "old-fashioned heroics," although the most professional poem Holmes ever wrote, "The Living Temple" (I, 175-76; 101-2), called by the Professor "The Anatomist's Hymn," was in octosyllabic couplets arranged in eight-line stanzas. It shares the wonder at the human body of Fletcher's "Purple Island," but it begins and ends with a tribute to the Divine Maker of "these mystic temples." The Professor also contributed the Class Poem for 1858, "Mare Rubrum," and the farewell to Motley of 1857.

But the professor's real triumph, again in the octosyllabic couplet, was "The Deacon's Masterpiece; or the Wonderful 'One-Hoss Shay'" (I, 252-56; 158-60), the success of which puffed him up ridiculously—until he found he could not repeat his success. Anyone familiar with New England dialect is delighted with the "Settler's ellum" that rhymes perfectly with "Couldn't sell 'em." The picturesque narrative is so entertaining that to lay on it a burden of allegory seems intrusive. But the dates of 1755 and 1855 are as carefully given as the proper wood for spokes and thills, crossbars and panels; and, reluctant as the reader may be to accept the tale as an account of the downfall of Calvinism, the stress on *logic*—the subtitle is a "A Logical Story" and the last line is "Logic is logic. That's all I say"—surely points in that direction, especially as the principle of Calvinism developed by Jonathan Edwards and rejected by Holmes was its irrefutable logic. This allegorical reading of the poem is the strongest argument that may be offered against Holmes's being "crippled" by his early orthodox exposure, as he had remarked a child brought up under the shadow of the doctrine of original sin must be. The wound was surely there; but, as Holmes often urged in his medical addresses, nothing is more healing than fresh air and sunshine, here the sunshine of wholesome laughter.

When *The Autocrat of the Breakfast-Table* appeared as a book late in 1859, it was warmly welcomed, as had been the numbers appearing in the *Atlantic Monthly*. It has been the most popular of Holmes's books, and generally regarded as best preserving the talk which his contemporaries maintained was more scintillating and delightful than any of his printed works. Henry James, Sr., told him once: "Holmes, you are intellectually the most alive man I know." As the first of its kind, it had the advantages of originality of form, variety of subject matter, imaginative play with history and literature, and a warm familiar style which won loyal friends then and has continued to win them.[4]

II *The Professor*

The Professor at the Breakfast-Table suffered from being second on the scene, from being only the *alter ego* of the more lively Autocrat, and from too many serious openings like "I have a long theological talk to relate." As the Autocrat took his leave, hoping "you will love me none the less for anything I have told you," he announced that the Professor was to be his successor. That was in the *Atlantic* for October, 1858, but the Autocrat continued to appear in titles of articles for the November and December numbers in order to get the twelve numbers on a calendar-year basis, a program which the other two in the series and the novels followed. The titles in the November and December issues explained they were filling in: "A Visit to the Autocrat's Landlady" and "The Autocrat gives a Breakfast to the Public." When the Professor took over in January, 1859, a change was immediately apparent, particularly during the early numbers. The Professor tried to take up his subject, "the great end of being is . . . ," but was interrupted. A new boarder, a vulgar man with dyed hair and a diamond pin dubbed the "Kohinoor," was paying attention to the landlady's daughter; but these, the young man named John, and the divinity student—all are perfunctory and lifeless until the drama of the cripple Little Boston and the warm-hearted Iris develops.

Statements are still made memorable by brief figurative phrasing, as when the Professor replies to the divinity student's warning to stay off important subjects like religion: "Truth is tough. It will not break like a bubble at a touch; nay, you may kick it about all day, like a football, and it will be round and full at evening" (II, 109). Or when he notes wisely of the true artist: "A moment's insight is sometimes worth a life's experience" (II, 239). The Professor is careful to explain he does not call phrenology a pseudo-science; but he points out how it imposes on human gullibility, uses the name of Bumpus & Crane for his practitioners, and by the way they go through a group concludes "They go only by the bumps"—and is interrupted by the boarders' laughter. His incidental comment sometimes gives the same pleasure and surprise of recognition as the Autocrat's did so often, as when he notes we are all surprised by our own pictures; we think we know how we look, but "no genuine expression can be studied by the subject of it in the looking-glass" (II, 190). He also takes a shot at the portrayals of children in contemporary publications; "these tearful records of premature decay" is an apt summary of the popular engravings of ill or dying children in gift-books or the moral tales in a period when Poe gave us Annabel Lee and Harriet Beecher Stowe, little Eva.

Such apt and amusing comment is less frequent in *The Professor* than in *The Autocrat*; also less frequent are vivid scenes from Holmes's experience. An exception is the poem "The Opening of the Piano" (II, 73-74; 166-67), when Holmes takes us back to the family in the gambrel-roofed house as the "London-made piano" was opened to the eager cries of pushing children quieted by the grave father, and the mother's " 'Now, Mary, play.' "

The emphasis in this book is more serious and more theological, although in his first indictment the Professor links medicine with religion: homeopathy in medicine and spiritualism in religion are "out of the mouths of fools and cheats" and "the folly of the world . . . confounds the wisdom" (II, 13). The strong language called forth attacks in many church papers and caused some ministers to warn their congregations away from heresy. Many subscriptions to the *Atlantic* were cancelled, but not enough to worry the publishers. Holmes did make a scrap-book[5] out of the clippings sent to him or to the editor of attacks in newspapers or magazines; he did not, therefore, so entirely ignore them as he pretended in the prefaces he wrote later and in his refusal to answer.

The Professor uses strong language again when he adds law to medicine and religion: "The three learned professions have but recently emerged from a state of *quasi* barbarism." After citing examples of superstition and cruelty, with all too recent dates, he concludes that primal instincts are violated "when the ideas of the healing art, of the administration of justice, of Christian love, could not exclude systematic poisoning, judicial duelling, and murder for opinion's sake" (II, 105-6). In this book Holmes combines *logic* and Jonathan Edwards in a way which argues that the *logic* in "The Deacon's Masterpiece" did point to an allegory of orthodox Calvinism; after reference to the Northampton church's dismissing Edwards, he closes the paragraph: "A man's logical and analytical adjustments are of little consequence, compared to his primary relations with Nature and truth; and people have sense enough to find it out in the long run; they know what 'logic' is worth" (II, 114)—a phrasing only slightly different from "Logic is logic. That's all I say."

The Professor does not use merely the weapon of straight attack, however. Like Swift, Holmes made up names: *Bumpus & Crane* ridiculed phrenology; the *Muggletonians* are called to mind by the divinity student's stubborn dogma. But the figures still do the most to clarify and interest, as with the classification of Broad Church and Narrow. The latter is a garden fenced in; without a forcing system only plants of one zone—arctic, tropical, or temperate—will grow there together. More vivid is the contrast of Broad and Narrow in the figure of boats: the Broad working the pumps on board to save all; the Narrow "in the long boat, in the jolly boat, in the captain's gig, lying off the poor old vessel, thanking God that *they* are safe" (II, 296-98).

The theological issues become poignant and dramatic when they concern the cripple and Iris. The latter is a sensitive, beautiful orphan who has been given study and training in the city by her patroness, "the Model of all Virtues." Her week at the boarding house did not add to the enjoyment of any—"that excellent lady whose only fault was, that Nature had written out her list of virtues on ruled paper, and forgotten to rub out the lines" (II, 316). Holmes reminds us we must find "a weak spot or two in a character before we can love it much." The cripple's changing status in the group is indicated by his names: at first he is the Sculpin; as pity and respect for him grow but, as he harps on Boston as the Hub of the Universe and the view from the State House as unequaled for what is worth seeing, he becomes Little Boston; by the closing pages he is the Little Gentleman. He talks much about making our religion match our politics: "a man's soul has a vote in the spiritual community; and it doesn't do, Sir, or it won't do long, to call him 'schismatic' or 'heretic' and those other wicked names that old murderous Inquisitors have left us to help along 'peace and good-will to men'" (II, 207). After he has said we are battling for a new faith in the United States and the divinity student remarks it is late in the world's history to be looking for a new faith, his reply is consciously American: "I didn't say a new faith . . . old or new, it can't help being different here in this American mind of ours from anything that ever was before; the *people* are new, Sir, and that makes the difference" (II, 218). The Professor also expresses faith in our national growth toward more freedom from Old World traditions and superstitions, and waxes eloquent with the vision:

Never, since man came into this atmosphere of oxygen and azote, was there anything like the condition of the young American of the nineteenth century. . . . heir of all old civilizations, founder of that new one which, if all the prophecies of the human heart are not lies, is to be the noblest, as it is the last; isolated in space from the races that are governed by dynasties whose divine right grows out of human wrong, yet knit into the most absolute solidarity with mankind of all times and places by the one great thought he inherits as his national birthright; free to form and express his opinions on almost every subject, and assured that he will soon acquire the last franchise which men withhold from man,—that of stating the laws of his spiritual being and the beliefs he accepts without hindrance except from clearer views of truth,—he seems to want nothing for a large, wholesome, noble, beneficent life. In fact, the chief danger is that he will think the whole planet is made for him, and forget that there are some possibilities left in the *débris* of the old-world civilization which deserve a certain respectful consideration at his hands (II, 284).

Walt Whitman was not the only American who had a vision and a faith during those politically troubled years before the firing on Fort Sumter. But Holmes's enthusiasm is rationally tied down by the play with scientific terms for *atmosphere* at the beginning and by the wry warning at the end.

The romance between the young Marylander and Iris, as they sit nearer each other at table and walk together, is less tense and moving than the growing tenderness between the Little Gentleman and Iris. The high point, emotionally and theologically, is when the Little Gentleman is ill, probably fatally, and the Professor attends him while the divinity student prays for him. When he asks the Little Gentleman conventional questions about repenting of his human sins, the latter passionately denies having in any way shared the life of men in this world. His left arm alone has escaped the curse of crippling; its beauty of form and movement is often mentioned. It contrasts sharply with the misshapen body, where even the heart is misplaced: it is on the right side instead of the left. All he has ever known in his encounters with other mortals has been curiosity, repulsion, sometimes pity. As he ends his passionate avowal of how completely he has been isolated from all ordinary human experience, of his loneliness without love of man or caress of woman, Iris leans to kiss him, and is repaid by his grateful tears. Even the divinity student realizes "he could trust this crippled child of sorrow to the Infinite Parent" (II, 302), and he asks to pray with rather than for him.

The end comes quickly, with the Little Gentleman crushing Iris' hand in a last desperate struggle to make up for a lifetime of isolation from his kind. The mystery which has gathered about his rooms because of the strange sounds of heavy movements at night and of a human voice in pain is solved a trifle arbitrarily. During sleepless nights he relieved his suffering by sharing it with the loving Saviour on the Cross, whose statue he could not reach without pulling out a heavy cabinet; the voice in pain is the *vox humana* stop on the fine organ which he has willed to the Professor. Holmes's lively interest in musical instruments, especially in any new invention, is reflected here. The note of scientific curiosity is odd in the midst of slightly Gothic shadows and suspense. But this mixture of shadowy mystery with active contemporary curiosity counts less as an artistic flaw because all is relaxed and anticlimactic after the death of the cripple. One detail is stressed and carries symbolic tension: Little Boston had wanted a six-foot coffin and a grave to match so that, after death, he could take his place in the world of men without the blunted deformity he had carried while living. His wish is fulfilled and Iris' annual return from Maryland to visit that grave, later with children, leaves all happily taken care of at the end.

It is appropriate to the prevailingly serious tone of the arguments and the dramatic intensity of Little Boston's proud struggle that the two best-known poems from this book are hymns. Iris' tender "Hymn of Trust" (II, 282; 163), "O Love Divine, that stooped to share / Our sharpest pang, our bitterest tear," has brought surcease from pain to others besides Little Boston, with its closing "Content to suffer while we know, / Living or dying, Thou art near." At the end the Professor asks all his readers—the friends and the vexed alike—to join in singing his hymn to "the warmth that alone can make us all brothers." It is called "A Sun-Day Hymn" (II, 319; 163-64), and begins "Lord of all being! throned afar"; the lines most characteristically Holmes's are "Lord of all life, below, above, / Whose light is truth, whose warmth is love." Less devotional than the other, it has become one of the great hymns of the Protestant church.[6]

The subtitle of *The Professor* was changed for book publication in 1860. In the magazine under the title had been, in italics, "What he said, what he heard, and what he saw." In his farewell remarks the Professor made reference to this: "The Professor has talked less than his predecessor, but he has heard and seen more," a fair estimate of the way interest shifted from the talk of the Professor to the tender relations between the cripple and Iris. It was artistically fitting that the subtitle in the book be changed to "With the Story of Iris."[7]

III *Medical Lecturer*

Chronologically and thematically a medical lecture, "Currents and Counter-Currents in Medical Science," deserves mention. On May 20, 1860, Holmes addressed the Annual Meeting of the Massachusetts Medical Society, and he argued as eloquently against entrenched ignorance in medical practice as the Professor and Little Boston had argued against the narrow fencing-in by creeds in religion. He first exposed the delusion doctors suffered when they supposed they were treating their patients according to the techniques of experience. All too often the treatment was based merely on some prevalent fashionable belief which was accepted without testing because it had prevailed for so long. He warned the physician who prided himself on being a practical man and on leaving mere theorists to watch the currents of progress that he needed to look out and up and find out where he was going. Colorful examples are introduced of an arctic expedition on which no traveler would have known he was traveling backward if he had not lifted his eyes from the track; of the workman who covered the niche in the wall without noticing the human figure within; of the Jewish artisan who nailed together two pieces of timber for Pontius Pilate. Then these examples are pointed home in one sentence: ". . . with subtler tool than trowels and axes, the statesman who works in policy without principle, the theologian who works in forms without a soul, the physician who, calling himself a practical man, refuses to recognize the larger laws which govern his changing practice, may all find that they have been building truth into the wall, and hanging humanity upon the cross" (IX, 176-77).

The fact that there was a closer relation between the medical sciences and the prevailing social and political thought of a period than most people realized, was made persuasive—as had been his previous handling of "Homeopathy and Its Kindred Delusions,"—by his beginning with examples far enough in the past to be seen objectively. Andreas Vesalius was linked with Luther in his defiance of a church authority that forbade investigation and protected corruption; Marie François Xavier Bichat's practice caused as great an upheaval in surgical circles as Napoleon's in military and political ones; Dr. Benjamin Rush, who emancipated American medicine from slavish following of European practices, was a contemporary of men who founded a new nation.

Holmes prepared his audience psychologically for what he wanted it to give undivided attention to. "The more positive knowledge we gain, the more we incline to question all that has been received without absolute proof" (IX, 181). Homeopathy and Spiritualism were paired, as they were in *The Professor*, as caves of folly to which the frightened retreated when their old beliefs were threatened. But the real target here was overmedication, the resort to drugs and specifics with no attempt to find out the causes in order to prevent the diseases. Hippocrates' distinction between Nature and Art—what the body will do on its own and what should be done by the attending doctor—was traced through the centuries as it had been passionately defended or as passionately denounced. Dr. Rush was cited again and his denunciation quoted; his connection with the American Revolution was used with different effect from the first citation: the huge doses he prescribed were as "heroic" as the times in which he lived. Holmes was too serious here to indulge in the colloquial or the amusing, but the witty turning of the coin to see both sides marked poise of intellect rather than unleashed invective. He recommended the life and writings of Rush to the student who wished "to understand the tendencies of the American medical mind, its sanguine enterprise, its self-confidence, its audacious handling of Nature, its impatience with her old-fashioned ways of taking time to get a sick man well" (IX, 192).

Although the science of semantics would not be born till the next century, Holmes was practicing it when he pointed out the need to find workable definitions for words that had become emotionally confused such as *Nature, Art, Disease, Food, Medicine, Physic*; he went on to offer such definitions (IX, 196-97). One attack sounds like a page out of today's newspaper: "Add to this the great number of Medical Journals . . . many of them excellently well conducted, but which must find something to fill their columns, and so print all the new plans of treatment and new remedies they can get hold of . . ." (IX, 193-94). A modern reader misses only the stress on the income from advertising which paves the way for quack remedies in large type. After several examples of widespread misuse of such drugs as opiates, Holmes recommended the following for consideration: "The *presumption* always is that every noxious agent, including medicines proper, which hurts a well man, hurts a sick one" (IX, 201). He cited his experience as physician at the Boston Dispensary as his chance to learn that "medication without insuring hygienic conditions is like amputation without ligatures" (IX, 203).

In his closing words Holmes exhorted his "friends and brothers in Art . . . to save all our old treasures of knowledge and mine deeply for new, . . . to stand together for truth." Self-governing Americans were reminded that our history, unlike the Old World's, was not a history of "mounted majorities, clad in iron," but of a land where "the majority is only the flower of the passing noon, and the minority is the bud which may open in the next morning's sun." The attack here on traditional authority not tested by close and constant observation is the characteristic attack of Holmes the scientific thinker: he used as an example of failure to study actual cases the opposition to "The Contagiousness of Puerperal Fever." But his respect for the great medical works of the past was, as the word *treasures* indicates, more than intellectual respect; it was combined with a lover's delight in old books and a collector's joy in knowing their fine points.

> Shall I ever forget that rainy day in Lyons, that dingy bookshop, where I found the Aëtius, long missing from my Artis Medicae Principes, and where I bought for a small pecuniary consideration, though it was marked *rare*, and was really *très rare*, the Aphorisms

of Hippocrates, edited by and with a preface from the hand of Francis Rabelais? And the vellum-bound Tulpius, which I came upon in Venice, afterwards my only reading when imprisoned in quarantine at Marseilles, so that the two hundred and twenty-eight cases he has recorded are, many of them, to this day still fresh in my memory. And the Schenckius,—the folio filled with *casus rariores*, which had strayed in among the rubbish of the bookstall on the boulevard,—and the noble old Vesalius with its grand frontispiece not unworthy of Titian, and the fine old Ambroise Paré, long waited for even in Paris and long ago, and the colossal Spigelius with his eviscerated beauties, and Dutch Bidloo with its miracles of fine engraving and bad dissection, and Italian Mascagni, the despair of all would-be imitators, and pre-Adamite John de Ketam, and antediluvian Berengarius Carpensis, —but why multiply names, every one of which brings back the accession of a book which was an event almost like the birth of an infant? (IX, 410-11)

I quote these remarks here, which are from his Dedicatory Address at the Opening of the Boston Medical Library on December 3, 1878, because they convey so vividly the loving attention he lavished on medical works of the past, estimating justly their excellences and their mistakes. The purchases he was recounting in intimate detail were made during his study years in Europe, more than forty years before. Hence the warning sounded to students in the medical sciences in 1860 arose from a deep-seated concern for human welfare, not from impatience with the past or personal desire for novelty or notoriety. Although "Currents and Counter-Currents in Medical Science" was printed by the society in June, opposition to Dr. Holmes's stand arose: at an adjourned meeting on May 31, Dr. Childs of Pittsfield introduced a motion that "the Society disclaim all responsibility for the sentiments," and it was passed by a vote of nine to seven. The implied censure was recalled at a regular meeting on October 3, 1860, by a vote of twenty-seven to seventeen. Dr. Holmes was not disturbed by this opposition as he had been when authorities attacked his diagnosis of puerperal fever; nor did he need to be, for the doctors he respected shared his convictions and applauded his vigor and leadership. This serious professional address by Holmes at a time when he was capturing a large lay audience with his essays in the *Atlantic* illustrates the facility with which he moved from one area to the other.

Examples and analogies are no more picturesque and only slightly more frequent for the lay reader. If anything, the concentration and close thought of the medical address lend it as much interest and even greater force.

IV *The Poet*

Holmes's next two long writings for the *Atlantic* were novels, *Elsie Venner* and *The Guardian Angel*. The Autocrat had stated that every man has at least one novel in him; the direction *The Professor* had taken *With the Story of Iris* had given him a taste of the excitement which might await him, and his alert mind was always eager to branch out into new fields of human study. I shall consider the novels together in the next chapter, since they, like the three books of the Breakfast-Table series, share features which emerge more clearly when examined comparatively.

The Poet at the Breakfast-Table did not begin in the *Atlantic* until January, 1872, and it was published as a book at the end of that year. Besides the two novels in the 1860's *Soundings From the Atlantic* appeared in 1864—a collection of essays reprinted from the magazine. Three of the articles have been mentioned previously in connection with the Civil War: "Bread and the Newspaper," "My Hunt After 'The Captain,'" and "The Inevitable Trial." The last-named oration of July 4, 1863, had not appeared in the *Atlantic* because it had been immediately printed separately and widely distributed. Other essays dealt with new inventions which had caught Holmes's interest, usually through their similarity to natural processes of the human anatomy or of the natural world. Thus the titles of two of the three essays dealing with photography used "sun": "Doings of the Sun Beam" and "Sun-Painting and Sun-Sculpture"; the other was about the stereoscope, the use and study of which Holmes found so absorbing that by 1868 he had investigated "The History of the American Stereoscope." The subtitles of two essays explained the analogies he developed: "The Great Instrument: The organ in the Boston Music Hall, with a brief description of the anatomy of the human ear" and "The Human Wheel: The Physiology of Walking."

Occasional poems were still called for, and from farther away or for more distant celebrations. Besides appearing with Liszt, the piano virtuoso, and Ole Bull, the violinist, at Boston's overblown Peace Jubilee in June, 1869, he wrote poems for two anniversaries in Germany: President Barnard of Columbia University asked him to contribute to the Fiftieth Anniversary of Ehrenberg as Doctor of Medicine in November, 1868, and in 1869 Holmes and Agassiz helped make Boston aware of the centennial of the birth of Friedrich Humboldt. The subtitle of Holmes's poem "Humboldt's Birthday" (213-14) showed him still drawing a parallel between medicine and politics, "Bonaparte, August 11, 1769.—Humboldt, September 14, 1769." In 1869, Holmes was one of the members of the Massachusetts Historical Society who gave the Lowell Institute Lectures. His lecture, "The Medical Profession in Massachusetts," took him again to Colonial records, but he developed the relation between local practices and the general state of medical science instead of proceeding as he had with intermittent fever to a narrow but substantially supported conclusion—a contrast between broad and narrow that he had illustrated in religion in *The Professor* and that he would investigate in science in *The Poet*.

The inauguration of a new president at Harvard in 1869, Charles William Eliot, had brought the new emphasis on specialization into Holmes's professional life; he was made Professor of Anatomy, and Physiology was set off in a field of its own. President Eliot, who was affecting all people connected with Harvard, was "proposing in the calmest way to turn everything topsy-turvy," according to Holmes. Although Holmes was suspicious of the new emphasis on more lectures in the medical school instead of so much clinical work as he advocated, his position was more moderate than belligerent, and he wanted to reconcile the opposing sides. This position is echoed in the ambivalent arguments delivered in *The Poet*. Another personal effect *The Poet* echoed was the sale of the Holmes house in Cambridge to Harvard to make way for Eliot's program of change and of building which was soon to change or convert many familiar landmarks.

The necessity of cleaning out the old gambrel-roofed house took John and Wendell and Ann Upham back to the old days. The memories that found their way into Holmes's writing were published in the *Atlantic Monthly* in January of 1871 and 1872. The first was the poem "Dorothy Q." (186-87), delightful in its combination of pride, humor, and tenderness caught in quick rhyming couplets, about the portrait whose "rent the light shines through." He had learned as a child that the rent was made by a British "Redcoat's rapier thrust." He included early in the new book in the Breakfast-Table series his essay on "The Gambrel-Roofed House and its Outlook" (III, 10-31), and in it he not only indulged his own pleasure in going over experiences of his early years but also sketched a vivid and valuable picture of the old village Cambridge had been.

The immediate opening of *The Poet* identified some of the people now at the Breakfast-Table, which had been out of sight for twelve years: the gently satirized "Member of the Haouse" with his dialect and huckleberry-conscious constituents; the six-year-old Boy, whom the Poet refused to call *Bub*, because he knew that was the diminutive of *Beelzebub;* the Old Master, who had prejudices strong enough to rub against; and the Landlady, who was always interrupting. The Poet used her interruptions to introduce a comic literary interlude, like the Professor's Houhynhym Gazette, in which Shakespeare was imagined being likewise interrupted by Anne's query about his preference for pudding or flapjacks today when he was in the midst of composing Hamlet's "To be or not to be" speech. The looser organization of this book is one reason its effect is more diffused. The essay on early Cambridge comes before the introduction of the opponents of the Old Master; they are the scientists called the Scarabee and the Young Astronomer, and their absorption in special studies means narrow living and narrow loving. The Lady and Scheherezade appear later and are less sharply contrasted than the other feminine pairs. Holmes is determinedly seeing good in the young who are breaking up the old patterns. The Young Girl's being called Scheherezade has the old refreshing play: she too keeps herself alive by telling stories—only hers are sold to newspapers and magazines, a far cry from any Arabian nights. She differs from the Lady only in background and in enjoying the scientific discussions the latter finds tiresome and distressing. The link with the earlier books is managed through the Landlady and her family. Her daughter is now married to an undertaker, a cheerful soul when not on professional duty, and the Landlady goes to live with her when she gives up her boarding-house at the end. Benjamin Franklin has become a medical doctor, and Holmes ridicules him for his enthusiasm about all the new gadgets in his profession and for insisting on getting every detail of his patient's history before he will venture a diagnosis—Dr. Holmes laughing at the medical innovations he had proudly brought back from Paris, as he had earlier invited laughter at himself in "The Stethoscope Ballad." Minor figures like the Register of Deeds, the Capitalist, and Mrs. Midas Goldenrod (who takes up with the Lady again as soon as the Register of Deeds has restored her wealth by finding an old paper) remain names for dominant traits rather than human beings.

An inner circle is composed of the Old Master, the Poet, the Young Astronomer, the Scarabee, and occasionally Scheherezade. The Young Astronomer's poem "Wind-Clouds and Star-Drifts" closes seven chapters and is written in blank verse; both the form and the subject matter are attempts by Holmes to present sympathetically a reconciliation of his "narrow" and "broad." The compromise is only dimly etched in; the real life is in the Old Master and the Scarabee. The Young Astronomer may be a failure because of Holmes's lack of conviction or because he was trying to understand and interpret a young man near and dear to him, his son Oliver Wendell Holmes who was pursuing an independent course of life with marked success, was devoted to his law profession and was writing brilliant studies based on close and concentrated analysis, and who was rescued from lonely eccentricity by his brilliant wife and their richly shared social relations. The Poet gives an accurate estimate of the book when he is reflecting on the doubt the Lady expressed as to "whether she would find better company in any circle she was like to move in than she left behind her at our boarding-house. I give the Old Master the credit of this compliment. If one does not agree with half of what he says, at any rate he always has something to say, and entertains and lets out opinions and whims and notions of one kind and another that one can quarrel with if he is out of humor, or carry away to think about if he happens to be in the receptive mood" (III, 297).

The Old Master has an occasional epigrammatic sentence: "Sin, like disease, is a vital process" (III, 306). An elaborate figure he develops to illustrate "broad" and "narrow" is emotionally slanted: the eagle's flight leaves no track while the patient mollusc's boring into a marble column outlasts the temple. He sees it as a just picture of his ranging far and wide to investigate the "Order of Things" in contrast to the Scarabee's confining himself to beetles and thereby leaving a single point "finally settled for the instruction and, it may be, the admiration of all coming time" (III, 251-52). The Old Master summarizes Holmes's treatment of new inventions in *Soundings*: "There are many modern contrivances that are of as early date as the first man, if not thousands of centuries older" (III, 322-23). Telescope and microscope are related to the human eye, instruments to the larynx, and the new heating apparatuses of furnace and radiators to the human frame. Like the Professor, he is interrupted in his statement *"The one central fact in the Order of Things which solves all questions is,"* and when the Young Astronomer and the Poet want him to give his conclusion, he replies it is all there in his books and advises them to reach individual conclusions with a characteristically colloquial figure of speech: "It's quite as well to crack your own filberts as to borrow the use of other people's teeth" (III, 339; 344).

The vivid colloquial language and memorable figure are less frequent in *The Poet* than in earlier works; nevertheless the Poet's classification of men into one-story, two-story, and three-story intellects has been echoed so often, with or without attribution, that it may justly be named one of his famous figures. Its clarity and brevity are part of its power: "All fact-collectors who have no aim beyond the facts, are one-story men. Two-story men compare, reason, generalize, using the labors of the fact-collectors as well as their own. Three-story men idealize, imagine, predict; their best illumination comes from above, through the skylight" (III, 43). Some librarians are noted as examples of the one-story mind which stops at the fact; lawyers, as examples of the two-story; poets, of the three-story, "full of light, if sometimes rather bare of furniture, in the attics." The colloquial humor placed at the end to relieve the sharp classifications, would seem desirable for a man who made lawyers second-story intellects when his mother's father was a distinguished judge, his wife's father was equally renowned as a judge in his day, and his eldest son was already exhibiting, besides an intense devotion to his work, a range of imaginative thought and phrase and a poise of intellect which could employ the comic to advantage. For three decades of the twentieth century these characteristics would make the name Oliver Wendell Holmes mean to the public the brilliant judge and legal writer.

Though the Old Master sets the tone of the book and we are at home with him in his library, or reading from his published book or his new notes, no such emotional quickening takes place as Little Boston and Iris gave to *The Professor*. The Scarabee lives his part, and does finally manage one smile, but his correspondence is only with professional colleagues who are suspected as competitors eager to publish their papers ahead of his, and only his spider loves him. He and the Young Astronomer often refer to Darwin, and to the great logical advantages to be found in his theory of species as contrasted to the universe conceived in the Old Testament. Our national love of display is ridiculed, but gently, as when the Poet admits to the inordinate pride he takes in wearing a tiny parti-colored ribbon in his buttonhole. The most amusing puncturing of the inflated diction that Holmes, like Mencken later, finds characteristic of our national vainglory, is the Scarabee's *Muscarium*, which he explains is "my home for house-flies" (III, 244). A reference is made to the crusade for women's rights, but it is only gently satiric. There may be humorous diction or an incongruous comparison, but the tone is never one of attack or satire.

Besides the seven parts of the long poem the Young Astronomer is working on, the Poet closes his return to the gambrel-roofed house with the tender and comforting "Homesick in Heaven." The Angel is gentle as he helps the mourners seeking earthly forms in Heaven to comprehend that these forms belong only to the earth left behind. Only two poems offer comic relief. In "Aunt Tabitha" (III, 87-88; 171), Scheherezade makes Aunt Tabitha's manners amusing "When *she* was a girl (forty summers ago) . . . How wicked we are, and how good they were then." The book closes with an "Epilogue to the Breakfast-Table Series: Autocrat—Professor—Poet. At a Book store. *Anno Domini* 1972" (III, 349-51; 183-84). A passerby stops to look through "Your choice among these books, 1 Dime," and finds "A Boswell, writing out himself. . . . One actor in a dozen parts . . . Thy years on every page confessed . . . Thy hopeful nature, light and free, / I start to find myself in thee." His start of recognition makes him take all three, but he puts them in a class we also recognize: "Read you,—perhaps,—some other time."

At least for *The Autocrat* this prediction was wrong. In *The Poet* Holmes has talked frankly with his readers about the likelihood that the series will now have a diminished audience: he follows this by deciding he will take advantage of it and be more intimate with his one reader.[8] The first time this one reader is addressed as "Beloved," the effect is disconcerting, but gradually the reader begins to enjoy it. The tone is frequently less intimate than in *The Autocrat*—necessarily so when serious speakers and subjects are present—but it is as easy and more tender. The form is less developed, for fewer characters are brought to life and divisions are acknowledged and named; the range is narrowed and the sparkle dimmed. The Old Master and the Scarabee are alive and appealing each in his way, but the solution by way of the Young Astronomer is dim and contrived. He is saved from the lonely fate of the Scarabee by marrying the alert and independent Scheherezade, but his problem, variously presented in "Wind-Clouds and Star-Drift,"[9] remains the dilemma of the scientific humanist: to dedicate himself utterly to his work and, like the Scarabee, become important only to and for his beetles; or to respond freely to all living situations and creatures and to be welcome, like the Old Master, in any group because he wears his learning lightly, is tolerant, humorous, and wise. Little wonder that Holmes, by 1872 a confirmed occasional poet, skillful lecturer, and popular essayist, gave the Old Master all the advantages—except the lasting renown of a single achievement.

CHAPTER *4*

Three Novels

HOLMES'S NOVELS were written with a purpose; he was often specific enough in his mention of their purpose to leave no room for doubt. He wanted to soften judgments of deviations in behavior through recognition of physical and psychical limitations which require understanding and cure rather than condemnation. He accepted the term "medicated novels" applied to them by a "dear old lady," and he saw reason in her refusal to read them. In his novels Holmes focused attention on figures who had suffered psychological crippling by inheritance or childhood shock; he carefully outlined and analyzed the automatic actions to which these people were subject.

For the layman Holmes took up the subject of *Mechanism in Thought and Morals*[1] in a Phi Beta Kappa oration delivered at Harvard on June 29, 1870, after two and before the third of the novels had been published. The aspects of moral responsibility that demanded his attention in the novels were expounded and illustrated with more concentration in the oration. A brief introductory note explains that "the highly colored rhetoric" has been adopted for a spoken address; his treatment is to be "a wide range of suggestive inquiry, meant to stimulate rather than satiate the interest of the listener" as opposed to "that more complete treatment of a narrowly limited subject which is liable to prove exhaustive in a double sense." This awareness of audience response reveals the successful susceptibility to it. Holmes's confessed liking for popular acclaim probably contributed as much as any single factor to changing the devoted concentration on medical science of the youthful student in Paris to the attacks on narrow specialization of the medical professor. In *Mechanism in Thought and Morals* he preferred broad interests to narrow ones, just as he had favored the Old Master over the Scarabee and the Young Astronomer in *The Poet*.

Because certain processes of thought are genuinely mechanical, the idea of an individual's moral responsibility for all his actions is falsely mechanical and results in "mental confusion . . . in the sphere of morals" (VIII, 264), a startling reversal of the surface impression of the title. From experiences familiar to us all, such as trying to recall a detail in vain and then having it occur to us unexpectedly, Holmes goes on to examine thought somatically and to distinguish between what we can control and what comes to us automatically. That plagiarism is often unconscious he illustrates by citing similar phrases in a wide range of authors who have been treating of the same ideas—and incidentally displays a proper amount of accurate learning for a Phi Beta Kappa orator.

Holmes defines the moral universe as that which "includes nothing but the exercise of choice" (VIII, 301); hence it is in a totally separate sphere from action we cannot control. Choice naturally involves freedom of the will—and his old opponent, Jonathan Edwards. He labels the logic of Edwards, which concludes the will is not free, "the mechanical doctrine which makes me the slave of outside influences." The doctrine of "transmissible responsibility" is mechanical and brings moral chaos, since no man is master of his inherited tendencies. Theological dogma which finds "a scale of equivalents between moral choice and physical suffering" he labels a further "movement in moral materialism" (VIII, 306). Eloquently he urges emancipation from Asiatic modes of thought with medieval interpretations: "Does not the man of science who accepts with true manly reverence the facts of Nature, in the face of all his venerated traditions, offer a more acceptable service than he who repeats the formulae, and copies the gestures, derived from the language and customs of despots and their subjects?" As much as Whitman, Holmes rejoices in the freedom of the nineteenth-century American to challenge tradition; he values especially the "new type of religious character" that political freedom inevitably generates (VIII, 309-11).

He gives some memorable examples of the moral confusion that arises from trusting inherited belief instead of practical evidence: the earlier inhuman treatment of lunatics, "the most to be pitied of all God's children"; the rejection of evolution

because of confinement within rigid theological creed by Philip
Gosse, father of Edmund, that makes him take a fossil skeleton
by itself "—a kind of stage-property, a clever cheat, got up by
the great Manager of the original Globe Theater." Ignorance is
presumptuous and truth is humble. His remarks on each succeeding generation's swallowing and digesting the previous one
as a natural step in progress has a special relevance to the three
generations of Holmeses of which he was the second. His own
painful reaction against the crisis of doctrine the Reverend
Abiel Holmes was forced into in Cambridge was a deeper
wound than Oliver Wendell Holmes, Jr., gave any sign of
suffering as a result of being brought too near the public image
that Dr. Oliver Wendell Holmes was increasingly dependent
on in the last five years of his life when he was living with
his son and his wife, and father and son may each have had
too easy access to the other's "side-door." Intellectually at least
O. W. Holmes, Sr., welcomed the new generation and knew the
old must accept change: "Civilized as well as savage races live
upon their parents and grandparents. Each generation strangles
and devours its predecessor" (VIII, 312). This gaily serious call
to the young men he is addressing comes just before he closes
with references to three authors who lived close to human
nature and rendered it truly—Charles Dickens, Robert Burns,
and Nathaniel Hawthorne who "vindicated humanity, not against
its Maker, but against itself" (VIII, 313).

Unfortunately Holmes's appreciation of Dickens did not help
him to attain Dickens' skill in characters. But the wise old talker,
whose original was the Autocrat, appears in all three novels and
has an endearing vitality. Even incidental characters are convincing as picturesque or humorous figures familiar to New
England village life of the nineteenth century. All three novels
are set in New England villages, for the colorful and accurate
details of which Holmes could call on his memories of old
Cambridge, Andover, Hanover, and Pittsfield. The focus of
all the novels is a young person who is subject to a powerful
tension which controls action and reaction suddenly and power-
fully. All three are motherless, but Elsie Venner has a father,
and Maurice Kirkwood has known his father. In all three novels
Holmes stops to write essays on human affairs, to probe into a
nervous state and produce comparable examples from earlier
medical records, or to speak up against laying a burden of normal

responsibility on those psychically crippled by inheritance or experience.

I Elsie Venner

The first novel, *Elsie Venner: A Romance of Destiny*, under the title of *The Professor's Story*, began in the *Atlantic Monthly* in January, 1860, immediately after the last number of *The Professor at the Breakfast Table* in December, 1859. The link is less close than this title implies because the professor does not appear until the second chapter, and then only to recommend Bernard Langdon, his pupil at the Medical School, for the teaching position he is forced to take temporarily because of reduced family income. Even though Elsie Venner does not appear until the end of the fourth chapter, the change of title is artistically right because Elsie is the controlling theme of the book: her strange ways; the gradual answering of the questions which she and her behavior raise; the effect she has upon the normal people around her. The young man who is first introduced and whom we follow to Rockland and the Appollonian Institute for Young Ladies where he is at once struck by her strange beauty, helps to strengthen the story line of life-and-death which makes Elsie the central figure.

The opening chapter is an essay on "The Brahmin Caste of New England," through which Holmes developed an American meaning for the word *Brahmin*. That meaning was immediately stretched to apply to a class predominantly different from the one he intended, as More's *Utopia* has come to indicate something far different from the society he depicted. "Brahmin" has come to signify culture, taste, and elegance with a snobbish pride in lineage and a complacent condescension toward those less generously endowed with learning and family portraits; and it has helped Holmes earn the epithets of "snob," "provincial," and "genteel." Certainly he implies or expresses a regard for education, for intellectual attainments, and for a range of knowledge that is at home with the literary allusions all his works exhibit as the most natural way to enrich what he is saying for his readers. That this range of allusion offered added appeal to his contemporaries may or may not be construed as part of the eagerness of a new nation to absorb as fast and as widely as possible the learning and culture of the Old World; even in a twentieth century that would call itself more sophisticated,

Americans can scarcely be labelled subtle or discriminating in their scramble for culture. The Brahmin Holmes actually presents in this chapter is "the harmless, inoffensive aristocracy" with an "aptitude for learning" which is "congenital and hereditary" (V, 4).

Another feature of New England society Holmes recognizes and calls by its accepted name is "hired help." The pride and the independence of these workers are delightfully hit off in the person of Abel Stebbins, who works for Dr. Kittredge: "The Old World has nothing at all like him. He is at once an emperor and a subordinate. . . . Abel Stebbins, the Doctor's man, took the American view of his difficult position. He sold his time to the Doctor, and, having sold it, he took care to fulfil his half of the bargain. . . . When he came to live with the Doctor, he made up his mind he would dismiss the old gentleman, if he did not behave according to his notions of propriety" (V, [134]-136).

The society of Rockland village is divided according to houses: the mansion-house row and the two-story houses, genteel but not so comfortable as the honest farmhouses. Colonel Sprowle's tea-party is given in detail more amused than satiric. The Appollonian Institute had for a model the Young Ladies' Institute in Pittsfield where Holmes had given a poem. "The Mountain" which overhangs the town, and carries its menace of rattlesnakes and of the melodramatic avalanche Holmes brings in at the end, is Graylock—the same mountain Melville had faced as he created the ocean scenes in *Moby Dick*. Naturally Holmes devotes attention to ministers and churches. The Reverend Dr. Honeywood owes something to the Reverend Abiel Holmes in the contrast between his gentle, loving nature and the harsh creed of his church; and in his preference for sermons about a loving Saviour instead of those expounding a harsh dogma of original sin and eternal punishment. Like Holmes's father, Honeywood has to face up to a group in his church which disapproves his weakness on doctrine; unlike him, he goes happily and successfully with the liberal group and leaves the orthodox to make their painful way under Deacon Shearer in the church building the Reverend Chauncy Fairweather has left vacant when he succumbs to his yearning for the secure authority and regulated worship of the Roman Catholic chapel at the foot of the hill.

These details of village life and characters are needed before the girl Elsie and her snakelike characteristics are introduced.

Three Novels

Seeing her in relation to a normal village and its life makes the reader, like the villagers, accept her strangeness, wonder about it, and wait in suspense to learn her fate—and understand it. Her "diamond eyes" and seasonal languor or energy fascinate and frighten. Closest to her is Old Sophy, the Negress whose primitive instincts make her protective, sensitive, and far from the rational approach of the troubled and loyal father, Dudley Venner. Bernard Langdon is as uneasy as the father, and he writes the Professor of his experiences with this strange young girl.

The action concerns Elsie and her sudden violence and bewildering unpredictability. When Bernard Langdon has ventured too close to danger on Rattlesnake Ledge and the snake sounds its rattle, it is suddenly subdued by what Bernard discovers is the gaze of Elsie, who has come up silently behind him. Instinctively she is protecting the man to whom she has been drawn from a danger she knew and could save him from. Elsie's cousin Dick, who has been sent away earlier but who returns determined to wed Elsie and gain the Venner property, is the least convincing character in the book. Violent with his foreign trappings and dangerous horse and with his scheme of murdering his rival Bernard, he is effective only in his relations with Elsie, who will suddenly turn on him, when he presumes too far, with a violence that matches his. Holmes explains Dick only by the foreign blood of his mother and his residence in South America.

The sage old man who is turned to for understanding and help by all the figures in the actions which center in Elsie, is Dr. Kittredge, the village practitioner wise in human ways through years of experience. His "hired help" saves Bernard from Dick's night attack, and the doctor himself helps Dick to escape unobserved. After Elsie has asked for Bernard's love and lost her will to live because he gently puts her off, Dr. Kittredge asks the sensitive schoolmistress Helen Darley to stay with Elsie, till the leaves of the white ash seal her doom. The leaves are furnished by Bernard Langdon, his innocent contribution to the basket Elsie's schoolmates bring to her. Holmes admits he follows the old superstition that these leaves are fatal to rattlesnakes rather than his own close investigation of the rattlesnake kept for many months in the basement of the Medical School in order to study his reactions to prodding and to changes of temperature (Morse I, 258-59).

The moments when the snake in Elsie takes over are therefore accurate in detail as well as frighteningly vivid. The situation Holmes uses—a girl poisoned before birth by the bite of a rattlesnake her mother suffered the July before the October she was born and of which her mother died—he did not insist upon medically. He welcomed the examples he had heard or read of before and was notified of after, but only for their making his story more plausible—"as a convenient medium of truth rather than as a scientific conclusion" (V [vii]). He denied the influence of myth or fable or of Keats's *Lamia*, and he summed up his thesis as "a physiological conception fertilized by a theological dogma" (V, x). But the snake in Elsie, kept primarily to the physical and emotional and realized most through the effects on outside observers—on Dudley Venner, on Sophy, on Helen Darley, on Bernard Langdon—exerts a persistent fascination not matched by woman and snake in literature since Eve.

Holmes's first novel drew a range of comment—from Whittier's finding the conception of Elsie "one of the most striking in all romance," through essays linking him with Rabelais and Goldsmith as another doctor who wrote fiction, to sharp attacks in church papers. After *The Professor* had alerted the orthodox to the many ways Holmes was pointing out how little dogma and strict creeds had to do with genuine Christianity, religious newspapers had begun warning their readers against him as dangerous, particularly for young readers. Certainly the Reverend Dr. Honeywood of *Elsie Venner* is contrasted with his more orthodox parishioners in a fashion which would alienate the latter. But in general Holmes is more temperate in the novel than in *The Professor*, and he even issues a warning against putting too much stress on the mechanical. Langdon's Professor warns him in his reply to all his queries about Elsie and her strange ways, of the danger of relying too much on "automatic action in the moral world. . . . People are always glad to get hold of anything that limits their responsibility" (V, 227-28). No modern reader would fear Holmes as heretic; on the contrary, his discourses on religious sects and practices seem less pertinent than his psychological study, with the possible exception of the Reverend Fairweather's turning to the authoritative worship of the Roman Catholic chapel with relief because a pattern was laid down and he did not have to form his own. The refuge in religion in Holmes's time was more apt to be spiritualism, and he had paired it with homeopathy in medicine as a cave in which the frightened took cover. The "medicated novel" is not shunned today; advances in psychology have educated a new audience for *Elsie Venner*.[2]

II *The Guardian Angel*

Although by 1864 Fields was asking Holmes for another American novel for the *Atlantic,* it was not until 1867 that *The Guardian Angel* began appearing as the leading piece in each number through the year. It was published as a book in November, in time for the Christmas trade, but its sale was only half that of *Elsie Venner*.[3] The reason is not far to seek: the heroine, Myrtle Hazard, comes before us far less often than she is talked about, and she never creates the haunting suspense that Elsie does. What drives Myrtle to strange behavior is the tension engendered by the oppressive sternness of a maiden aunt in a lonely country village when Myrtle, who was born in India, has carried within her memories of sunshine and tropical colors, of loving parents who died in a plague of cholera, and of a long, enchanting ocean voyage. Her strange behavior is also due to inherited traits that suddenly seize control of her actions—traits inherited from an Indian princess, a Protestant martyr burned at the stake under Queen Mary, a proud beauty of Colonial days, and a major of the Revolution. As Holmes in *Elsie Venner* suggested "the limitations of human responsibility" because of prenatal influence, he wanted to show in *The Guardian Angel* the "successive development of inherited bodily aspects and habitudes . . . well known to all who have lived long enough to see families grow up under their own eyes. The same thing happens, but less obviously to common observation, in the mental and moral nature" (VI, viii).

The opening of *The Guardian Angel* is more immediate than in *Elsie Venner.* The advertisement of Myrtle's disappearance rouses interest in her, even though Holmes does stop to give the general contents of a country newspaper before he gets to the advertisement. The wise old man is Byles Gridley, a retired professor and *Magister Artium,* whose book *Thoughts on the Universe* is the first appearance of the Old Master's *Order of Things,* as he is a prototype for the Old Master. He plays a part in the action that concerns Myrtle, and in other actions which distract attention from Myrtle and her plight. These distractions make the book less concentrated and less powerful than *Elsie Venner*, despite the linking of actions through Byles Gridley. It is Byles who goes to get Myrtle after she has been rescued from the river at the falls by Clement Lindsay; who saves her in her nervous state from a dangerous dependence, first on young Dr. Hurlburt, next on the Reverend Bellamy Stoker; who sends her away to school in the city at his expense; who foils the plot of ambitious lawyer Bradshaw and the susceptible female relative Cynthia Badlam to hide and use for their own purposes the paper which settles the old land-title in Myrtle's favor and would bring her wealth as chief heiress; and who counsels Susan Posey to set Clement Lindsay free from their early, mistaken engagement so that she can give her undivided worship to Gifted Hopkins, and he, his to Myrtle.

Gifted Hopkins is the young poet often published in the country newspaper; like his mother and Susan, he is convinced of his genius. His portrait and the tone Holmes takes here had been sketched in by the Autocrat: "I always think of verse-writers, when I am in this vein [of warning aspiring authors]; for these are by far the most exacting, eager, self-weighing, restless, querulous, unreasonable, literary persons one is like to meet with. . . . Just as my heart yearns over the unloved, just so it sorrows for the ungifted who are doomed to the pangs of an undeceived self-estimate" (I, 292). "The bard of Oxbow Village" and his effusions are presented by a practicing poet who knows all too well the temptations and dangers of authorship, and he makes Gifted's plagiarisms and trite figures thoroughly entertaining. Because of the ironically named Gifted's insistence, supported by his adoring mother—who has spent her life literally as well as emotionally supporting Gifted—Byles Gridley takes Gifted to his old publisher to get the unpleasant truth firsthand. The publisher's recognition of Byles Gridley's name because he has been wanting to bring out a new edition of his book is as pleasing to the reader as it is to Gridley; Holmes's own pleasure at the demand for his prose writings after 1857 warms the passage. References to the Civil War are both personal and topical: the shock that the firing on Fort Sumter brought to the village; the responses from Bradshaw and Gifted who find excuses not to go to war, in contrast to Clement Lindsay's immediate relinquishing of his art studies and duties to serve through to the end. Like Wendell, Jr., Lindsay was wounded more than once but always went back—not through any romantic heroism but because of stern duty. He too called war "organized barbarism."

Myrtle's tensions are psychologically more complex and less fearful than the prenatal poisoning which gives Elsie snakelike moments. Her nervous instability and resulting deviations are traced to childhood experiences which have left deep scars on an impressionable girl who is alone in an alien environment. Traits of ancestors she knows through portraits and sees in visions are also responsible for unpredictable behavior. Myrtle has and wears the gold bracelet which the proud Colonial beauty, Judith Pride, is wearing in the portrait that hangs conspicuously by the one of the martyred Ann Holyoake. These portraits have counted for more in Myrtle's conscious and unconscious life than the living inhabitants of the old mansion, Malachi and Silence Withers, Cynthia Badlam, and Kitty Fagan. Holmes uses "humour" names here and with the landlady and her daughter, Susan Posey, who is often compared to a flower in her fresh comeliness as she cleans the house.

Myrtle's experiences in the mansion with her alien living relatives are recounted by Holmes with close attention to psychological accuracy. One scar was left on the child's psyche at the age of three by Silence's determination to "break her will." Myrtle had refused to eat brown bread at supper, and asked for white. She was put in the attic to bring her to terms, and stayed there refusing to eat or drink for eighteen hours. Kitty Fagan, the warm-hearted Irish servant who is as convincingly natural as Holmes could make his incidental characters who did not carry the burden of a thesis, was Myrtle's only refuge in the house; she went to Byles Gridley when Myrtle needed more help than she could give or when she suspected harm was coming to the girl. In the first trial in the attic, Kitty brought the child down to her own bed, comforted her, and fed her. Myrtle's next experience in the attic was even more frightening: when she went up one day to explore, a hanging object was there, her uncle Malachi the miser, whose cold hand when she reached up to touch him in this curious position told her he was dead. The river she could look out on from her window became her dream of escape, and she planned her journey in the boat carefully, with the courage and love of adventure of the old Major. The sudden danger of the falls terrified her, and she was drowning when young Lindsay reached her and brought her to shore. He warmed her body by holding her to him, and he breathed into her mouth to restore her to life.

When Gridley brought Myrtle back to the mansion after Mrs. Lindsay had nursed her for many days, she was in a nervous state which Holmes again described with much detail of observation. Young Dr. Hurlburt proved the most welcome visitor; by his touch and voice she was soothed and restored. Bradshaw, the most stereotyped villain Holmes drew in any of his novels, feared another would gain power over Myrtle to defeat his schemes of getting her fortune, and reported to Gridley her reliance on the young man's physical presence. He went to the young doctor, frankly stated his fears for Myrtle, and suggested that the old doctor go in his place. When old Dr. Hurlburt replaced his son, Myrtle at first suffered from the loss of the presence that gave her peace. The next man to wield a magic power over her nervous excitability was less innocent than the doctor. The Reverend Bellamy Stoker is the ugliest picture of a minister Holmes ever drew because he is a hypocrite who uses his pastoral calling to indulge his sexual drives. Stoker had been called in as assistant to old Reverend Dr. Pemberton, who was another minister like the Reverend Abiel Holmes; he was human and gentle but trained in a rigid creed which he accepted without question.

But Stoker was not modelled after anyone from Holmes's adolescence: he was a mature investigator's study of many recently labelled sexual deviations, indicated further by Mrs. Stoker's persistent illness because her husband expended his passion in hell-fire sermons and tender interviews with young females and left her emotionally starved. Her daughter Bathsheba devoted herself to her mother with an adoration that troubled her normal friends and companions. Cynthia Badlam noticed with jealousy the tender attentions Stoker was now devoting entirely to Myrtle, whose beauty and exciting tales of visions she had of her parents, of her martyred ancestress, of the Indian princess whose blood ran in her veins, fascinated and stirred the "man of emotions" who "loved to feel his heart beat; he loved all the forms of non-alcoholic drunkenness" (VI, 158). Cynthia ran to Mrs. Hopkins, who sought out Byles Gridley. He went to Myrtle and helped her to see that Stoker's attentions were always centered on those of her age and sex. The chief ammunition Holmes gave his critics in this novel was the psychologically penetrating analysis of the Reverend Bellamy Stoker when he received Myrtle's note of dismissal after he had "made himself as captivating as his professional costume allowed" to receive her visit. His rage found expression only when "his savage mediaeval theology came to his relief" and he got out his tried and well-worn " 'convulsion-fit' sermon" (VI, 190-92).

Madame Delacoste's school in the city, where Byles Gridley arranged to send Myrtle, is a relief to the reader as well as to Myrtle. After the suffocating ugliness of the Stoker household with its psychologically twisted members, the topical satire on "sets" determined by the number of family estates, horses, and turnouts is in the tone of friendly, familiar ridicule. Myrtle's heredity helped her make a social evening's "tableau" of Pocahontas startlingly vivid—especially when a jealous rival snatched the wreath sent her and Myrtle gave an Indian's "battle-shriek" and stopped herself only just in time from stabbing the offender with the knife she was carrying to cut Captain Smith's cords. Less spectacular was the glow of confidence that came to her from Judith Pride's bracelet on her arm; she relied on that ancestress to see her through the society scenes a country girl would be bewildered by. As Dr. Hurlburt had colloquially put it to his son: "Live folks are only dead folks warmed over" (VI, 129).

Myrtle saw through the squabbles over her in the "small tattling community" after her stunning performance had brought her to the attention of parents and brothers. She preferred the plainly dressed girls "whose fathers did not sell by the cargo, or keep victualling establishments for some hundreds of people" to the "daughters of the rough-and-tumble millionaires who were grappling and rolling over each other in the golden dust of the great city markets" (VI, 271). Holmes was apparently counting on the protection of fiction to allow him a sharper attack than had been permitted at the breakfast-table on commercial fortunes that were pushing their way into the old society.

As social comment and psychological study, amazingly frank in its suggestions of sexual drives, the novel has amusing and memorable scenes and some convincing pictures of self-deception. But Susan Posey and Gifted Hopkins are followed more closely in their daily life than is Myrtle Hazard; Clement Lindsay is usually far away, only appearing as a kind of *deus ex machina* when Myrtle or Gridley or Susan needs help. Therefore it lacks the concentrated power of Elsie's plight, which is the focus of the chief scenes and characters.

III *A Mortal Antipathy*

Holmes's third and last novel, A *Mortal Antipathy*, was introduced by the essay "First Opening of the New Portfolio." He had retired from the Medical School in 1882, but the task he undertook in 1883 was more exhausting for him than his medical lectures. That task was a biography of Ralph Waldo Emerson, which he had been asked to write for the American Men of Letters Series; and, to the surprise of most people, including himself, he had accepted. It had meant devoting long hours to an author whose prose had never held for him the fascination it had for many who were less firmly rooted by temperament, training, and long habit, in the practical world of scientific fact. He was genuinely tired when the book was finished and published in December, 1884; but habit was strong, and in January, 1885, he opened the New Portfolio in the *Atlantic Monthly* with A *Mortal Antipathy*. The title is self-explanatory, as is everything else about the book: when there is the slightest chance of confusion—sometimes even when there isn't—an essay is produced on the subject. The village is called Arrowhead, the name of Melville's house south of the Wendell property in Pittsfield, but the name is connected with Indians and not with Melville. The important natural feature is the long lake, with Corinna Institute, a girls' school, at one end, and Stoughton University, a men's college, at the other. The central figure in this novel is a man, Maurice Kirkwood, who rouses village curiosity by remaining apart with his Italian servant Paolo. He has a mortal antipathy to women because a female cousin snatched him as a young child from his mother's arms, then let him fall into a thorny bush. Years later the mere sight of her had nearly felled him; hence he has avoided society to protect himself from possibly violent reactions to women.

The two girls of the story are never brought to life, nor is Kirkwood, but the pattern of meaning emerges clearly at all times. The names of the girls are "humour" names: Lurida

Vincent, called "the Terror" because of her avid zest for learning and a career to prove women the equals of men in every direction; Euthymia Tower, called "the Wonder" because of the coördinated rhythm of all her movements—physical, mental, emotional. The action begins with a race between the crews of the institute and the university; and in his account Holmes amuses himself and the reader by emphasizing the physical inequalities no amount of feminine determination can overcome. But time-worn feminine wiles still work, and the girls win because Euthymia throws out a flower to distract the men as they are making up the handicap—and her action is as much an echo from the classics as are the girls' names. Euthymia saves Kirkwood twice: literally, when she carries him, ill with typhoid, out of a burning building; then psychosomatically, when she marries him and so restores him that he can even meet his cousin without fear.

The Pansophian Society is the intellectual center of the town, and the author admits he would not have tried a novel if he had not had the papers read there to fall back on—a truth the reader realizes all too soon. Dr. Butts gives wise advice but is by no means so omnipresent as was Byles Gridley. Woman suffrage and women eager to move into new spheres of activity are emphasized through Lurida's untiring energies, but these are made a little silly only in contrast to Euthymia's poised perfection. Lurida wants to study medicine, and Dr. Butts gives Holmes's previous official view: women should not be forbidden to enter medical schools, but most would probably be happier as nurses. Dr. Butts also uses Holmes's published views on medical delusions in his paper for the Pansophian Society, and shares his admiration for Dr. Johnson. When Lurida is puzzled by Sydenham's advice to medical students to read and reread *Don Quixote*, Dr. Butts suggests the story of the young astrono-mer in Johnson's *Rasselas* as his idea of basic reading for the medical student. He closes his paper at the Pansophian Society:

> "Begin your medical studies, then, by reading the fortieth and the following four chapters of 'Rasselas.' Your first lesson will teach you modesty and caution in the pursuit of the most deceptive of all practical branches of knowledge. Faith will come later, when you learn how much medical science and art actually achieved for the relief of mankind, and how great the promises it holds out of still greater triumphs over the enemies of human health and happiness" (VII, 168-73).

A new and amusing facet of Holmes appears in the visiting literary celebrity. After the familiar warnings to aspiring authors, comes a bout between the celebrity and the interviewer who is going to get his man and his copy over any and all obstacles. Holmes is laughing at himself for never being firm enough to turn such people away; he always suffered acute distress when reports were not accurate, as they tended not to be save in the two publications he trusted, the Boston *Daily Advertiser* and the *Atlantic Monthly*. These two had learned to send him proofs; if there was not time for that, they were meticulous as to printing and accurate facts.

The leisurely ramble with his intimates Holmes had announced in opening the New Portfolio proved to be just that: *A Mortal Antipathy* emphasizes examples of antipathies and comments on them in relation to causes and cures. The crusade for women's rights has taken the place of religious dogma as a subject to be held up to disarming inspection. The contrast between Lurida's determined reading and inquiry and Euthymia's easy grace and helpful behavior as a woman is more real than are the characters of the girls. Lurida may have gained some aspects of reality from Holmes's early, unhappy acquaintance with the feminist Margaret Fuller, but Euthymia remains an idea in spite of proof of her existence by actions—and important actions.[4]

With the development of psychology and psychiatry as separate subjects with their own vocabularies, a professional interest in the cases Holmes presented with accurate detail as he described symptoms, diagnoses, and cures, has added a new dimension to his novels. A modern psychiatrist has found them "of sufficient importance as psychiatric and analytic studies of neuroses to warrant their re-presentation to sociologists and physicians"; "the social significance of mental deviation"[5] was conveyed by Holmes in his novels as it would be stressed in professional studies and in popular jargon during the 1930's. Because psychiatry so intimately touches upon human happiness and misery, the language it has formed has become public property, even though apt to be distorted rather than accurate. Therefore modern technical terms for conditions which may be identified by reason of Holmes's careful recording of minutiae[6] are worth noting. In all three novels the central figures exhibit the lack of control which is due to the operation of unconscious impulses and thought, the latter called by Freud *psychic determinism*. Elsie's case would be *schizophrenia*, because she has the symptoms of isolation, introversion, and self-indulgence. Her orgiastic dancing gave her the "liberation of repressed effects" that modern occupational therapy works to achieve. Her frozen state in church when the Reverend Fairweather fails to read her request for prayers resembles *catatonia*. Her death is *psychic suicide*: Bernard Langdon's inability to give her the love she asks for takes away her wish to live.

In Myrtle Hazard of *The Guardian Angel* may be seen many more clues to conditions identified by psychiatry. Her heightened awareness of ancestors and of her early years is called by Jung the *collective unconscious*. Her being successively Judith Pride or Ann Holyoake is an example of *alternating personality*. Finding her Uncle Malachi hanging dead in the attic gave her *psychic trauma*, and her vision on her boat-journey is *semi-hallucinatory*. Neurotic patients are often cured by Freud and Breuer by the *mental catharsis* afforded Myrtle by the young doctor and the Reverend Stoker. The latter's taking out his anger at losing Myrtle by preaching his "convulsion-fit" sermon is technically *displacement* and *overcompensation*. Mrs. Stoker's illness proceeds from *psychotic wish* rather than from any physical ailment. Myrtle's not recognizing Clement Lindsay but having an hysteric spasm is to be expected after the *amnesia* that followed the shock of their first meeting in the river. Lindsay's devoting himself to work on the statue of Myrtle is an example of *sublimation*. Finally Byles Gridley as the *Angel* of the title is rightly named; he corresponds to Freud's *superego*, the epitome of ideals and authority.

Maurice Kirkwood in *A Mortal Antipathy* is the most psychiatrically simple of the three. His *phobia*, fear of women, is the result of *psychic trauma*, easily identified by the *primal scene*, which is sexual in nature. Freud especially stressed infantile impressions as the cause of *neuroses*, and Maurice was only two years old when he was dropped by his cousin Laura. His recovery is due to *shock therapy*, but it is also sexual since Euthymia's arms and breast are what he is most conscious of. His being ill with fever at the time of the shock treatment is also sound: patients have been proven more susceptible to treatment when suffering from fever. Water may have many significances—in psychiatry as well as mythology. Myrtle's being beside, then on, and finally in the river lends itself to elaborate interpretation; Maurice's paper on ocean, river, and lake may be given Freudian readings of the subject's wish-relations with a universe of eternal forces.

I have noted these terms for the cases Holmes supplies not to present Holmes as a pre-Freudian, however much evidence might be assembled. He has made it clear that his interest in developing dramatic scenes of fiction involving characters suffering from mental and emotional strains is to investigate the causes behind misery and incomplete living and to point the way toward understanding, humane, and healing treatment instead of the punishments automatically demanded by religious and social conventions. Holmes was speaking for his own time in exposing the need for study of the human mind in relation to the body; he anticipated a future development in the thorough and perceptive study he made and presented of "mutual interactions of mind and body"—today the basis of psychosomatic medicine. In his last novel and in his oration of 1870, he was among the first to urge the investigation of human conduct by study of what he called "mechanisms in thought" and which today are called *neuroses*.

What modern psychiatrists applaud as Holmes's recognition of the functioning of sex in relation to mental tensions and their cure was noted with high disapproval in his own day. Church newspapers again focused directly on his exposures of un-Christian attitudes and sentiments masquerading as orthodoxy and traditionally accepted as such. Even a consciously modern and "liberal" paper like *The Nation* considered shocking his references to female bodies and his showing his heroines in their bedrooms. Certainly Holmes says nothing which would today be counted frankly anatomical; he severely criticized the details Zola and Whitman were presenting. He recognized such human ills and bodily functions as essential to the work of hospitals, but he thought literature no proper place for them. Sex is not named as such, but the relations between Elsie and Dick as well as between her and Langdon come through as being sexually stimulated; even more frank are the suggestions in Myrtle's relationships. Sex is really all there is to Euthymia, but she and the other main characters in *A Mortal Antipathy* fail to shock because they are so predominantly ideas discussed in essays.

CHAPTER 5

Friend and Guest of Honor, 1857-87

THE DIFFERENCE between contemporary interest in psychiatric or medical emphases in literature and the attitude of the nineteenth century is illustrated by an incident of Holmes's career when he combined medical knowledge with literary position. On December 15, 1859, the Massachusetts Historical Society held a special meeting to pay tribute to Washington Irving, who had been made an honorary member of the society and who had died on November 28. The *Proceedings* of the society (IV, 418-22) carried a full account of the conventional tributes paid by Edward Everett and Longfellow, as did the Boston newspapers. But Holmes's talk, which included parts of a letter written him by Irving's physician after Holmes had called on Irving on December 20, 1858, was only briefly summarized, with mere mention of medical details. Only one Boston newspaper, the *Courier* for December 19, 1859, gave his talk in anything like full detail. With Dr. Peters' permission, his letter of January 5, 1859, which gave a full account of Irving's symptoms for Holmes's comment, was also used in the *Courier*. When Holmes had read the letter at the meeting, the members were as humanly interested in an account of a personal visit and one doctor's report to another doctor as members would be a hundred years later: Holmes reported to Dr. Peters that the "members listened with great attention to the letter" and such attention surely influenced his subsequent decision to give it out for publication. The powerful nineteenth-century taboo against mention of physical detail, especially in connection with a famous author now ready for his pedestal, must have caused the amazing and disappointing reticence.[1]

Holmes gave as his chief reason for visiting New York the year before (December 17-24, 1858), his desire "to see and speak with Mr. Irving." Dr. Peters had sent him some of Irving's symptoms and various cures he had used for his asthma before Holmes left Boston. But it was not primarily as a doctor that he visited Irving, but as the author of *The Autocrat,* just out as a book and noted, then even more than now, as showing in its easy, felicitous prose, its ready humor, and its winning personal tone, a real kinship with Diedrich Knickerbocker and Geoffrey Crayon. Holmes considered "Sunnyside" as only less important for an American to visit than "Mount Vernon," esteeming Irving the Father of American literature as truly as Washington was of his country. Irving had discovered that *The Autocrat* "has a full, rich vein—so witty—and so much drollery," and he was eagerly following *The Professor* as it came out through 1859, even though his peripatetic nights had become "a strange gypsy and cat-like way of murdering good Christian sleep." Holmes went to New York "to deliver some lectures" and to be guest of honor at the Century Club. His host was Frederick S. Cozzens of Yonkers, and the entire occasion was one of many such which Holmes had not yet learned to refuse, although he was going to be forced to choose and reserve his energies as the years went on.

His visit to Irving, with the partly professional aspect Dr. Peters had requested of a medical professor and a fellow-sufferer from asthma, is one of two visits recorded of Holmes that mix the professional with the friendly and literary. The other "patient" was Hawthorne, who stopped at a hotel in Boston in 1864 after the shock of the death of his friend George Ticknor. The publisher had been traveling with Hawthorne in the hope that travel might restore the latter's health. Before Hawthorne went to New Hampshire to join ex-President Franklin Pierce, another friend who hoped travel would restore Hawthorne, Holmes visited "the great Romancer" at his stopping place and recognized that the end was near. Death came to Hawthorne on May 19, 1864, in Plymouth, New Hampshire, of the complete exhaustion of spirit, body, and mind which Holmes had known he could not prescribe for.

I *The Atlantic Breakfast*

So continuously was Holmes's life made up of occasions for which he wrote—and often delivered, if distance, time, and his health permitted—an ode, a hymn, an address, a dedication, or an appeal, that it is a relief to find him sometimes just visiting friends. J. Murray Forbes was frequently his gracious host on Naushon Island, although, characteristically, we know most about these visits from the poetic *jeux d'esprit* Holmes left behind. Charles Eliot Norton liked to have him in Newport in August, but asthma forced Holmes to cut short his visit in 1859, and after that he usually stayed close to Nahant, where many members of the Saturday Club spent their summers. In 1877, the Holmes family went to Beverly Farms, and the next year bought a house there, which was his address from July to September for the rest of his life. His identification with the *Atlantic Monthly* came to be as total as with the Class of '29 and the Saturday Club. James T. Fields and his wife Annie formed the center of a literary circle in Boston: at their house literary celebrities were entertained, and Holmes and his wife probably lived as intimately with them as with any family.

When the *Atlantic Monthly* celebrated Holmes's seventieth birthday with an "Atlantic Breakfast" at the Brunswick Hotel in Boston at noon on December 3, 1879 (for August 29), it was managed by the editor who had taken over from Lowell in 1867, William Dean Howells; Fields was unable to be present because he was lecturing fifty miles away. Even with all the notables present or sending messages, it was unthinkable that Fields should not be heard from. His allegory and Holmes's grateful note shed a light on the Holmes family which, for all the author's apparent intimacy with his readers, is kept severely out of his publications—save for the wartime outbreaks in connection with his eldest son's enlistment and being wounded, an outpouring easily attributable to the high tide of emotion and the common experience shared by many in the North. Although positive evidence is slight, everything points to Amelia Lee Holmes's being exactly what her husband called her, "the smartest and most capable of women." She helped keep the Autocrat a public image in which she had no part—unless the ubiquitous schoolmistress be a gay reference to the control she exercised.

Fields's allegory for the "Atlantic Breakfast" in 1879, began in the garden of a picturesque old house in Cambridge; a doctor was leaving and the light on the father's face revealed his joy at the birth of a son. The fairies decided they would try their magic even in this stern New England background, and they brought their gifts to the child: a sunny temperament and good cheer; the gift of song; pathos and romance subtly joined; eloquence to persuade and instruct; compassion and aid to the unfortunate. These qualities were to be expected, but the order has significance coming from an intimate friend with Fields's judgment. The next two gifts could be named only by so intimate a friend: ".... in due time he finds the best among women for his companionship, helpmeet indeed, whose life shall be happily bound up in his life"; "children worthy of their father, and all that a mother's heart may pray that heaven will vouchsafe her."

Holmes's reply, written on December 5, 1879, has a totally different tone from the flood of letters he wrote to express thanks, with appropriate quip or play, to the many celebrities who had paid him tribute. "I am not writing because I ought to, but because I cannot help it. You said two things Wednesday evening that no one else said, and which were all that were necessary to make my evening completely happy. Others said enough about me, as you did, and said it charmingly. But no one but yourself spoke of those who have made my life what it has been, and you have my heart-felt thanks for the delicate and tender way in which you put the sweetest flower of all in my evening's nosegay."[2]

II Memorials and Biographies

The gradual waning of Holmes's cherished wife's memory until by 1885 she had to have a companion to watch over her, and he a secretary to take care of the arranging and notes she had usually managed for him, meant a sadness which he did not publicly express or lament; only as memorials were asked from him did he allow the public image to admit sorrow. In 1874, he was called on for two such tributes: on April 29, his "Hymn" ("Once more, ye sacred towers," 215) was "sung by male voices" at the Memorial Services for Charles Sumner in Music Hall; on June 23, another "Hymn" (215) was sung at the Dedication of Harvard's Memorial Hall in Cambridge. Also in November, 1874, the *Atlantic Monthly* printed his "memorial outline" of his colleague at the Medical School, Professor Jeffries Wyman—so fitting an appreciation that the son, Dr. Morrill Wyman, ordered many offprints. In 1877, Holmes wrote for the *Daily Advertiser* an obituary for his son-in-law Turner Sargent, who had died on February 28. The death of his sister Ann Upham in April was a real break in the family circle, but he published nothing; she was not part of the public image—after she left "the gambrel-roofed house."

In September he prepared and presented before the Massachusetts Historical Society a "Tribute in Memory of Edmund Quincy and John Motley" which led him to develop his recollections of Motley into a *Memoir* which appeared in Boston and London in December, 1878. The brilliant historian and controversial diplomat who had suffered recall from Austria and humiliation in England at the hands of the country he served had been a valued friend and correspondent, especially during the last two decades, and what Holmes wrote was a passionate defense of his friend—one so passionate that parts of it were omitted from the publication in the *Proceedings of the Massachusetts Historical Society* as likely to be offensive to some of the important members who differed politically from Motley and personally from Holmes. The latter's sense of justice and his warm loyalty were quick and eloquent; but, as with his public arguments in the 1850's that abolition might prove more of a threat to the Union than slavery, he was naïve or blind about political currents and made his only serious mistakes when this naïveté showed up in his public utterances. Holmes's biography of Motley is a testimony to his loyalty and his deep admiration of the concentrated scholarship of a friend who grew into the exhaustive habits of work that Holmes had set as his own goal in his student days in Paris but had been tempted away from by public demand for the poet and the popular success of the essayist. Not a valuable study, except for the letters and the intimate details that bring the living man close, Holmes's constant praise weakens its final effect.

But the next biography Holmes wrote was undertaken under different circumstances. After Emerson's death in 1882, Holmes was asked to write his life for the American Men of Letters Series, and he gave the next years to careful study and preparation of the biography which appeared at the end of 1884. The reasons he decided to undertake this task were many. The most obvious was that in November, 1882, he had given his farewell lecture at the Medical School, "Some of My Early Teachers," and he looked forward to time for his own writing. Young Wendell's admiration for Emerson may have stimulated his father's curiosity and desire to make his own attitude at least informed. Finally, with his books about Motley and Emerson, Holmes could know that he had fulfilled one of Dr. Johnson's requirements for a biographer: that he be one who had lived close to his subject and had known him in his familiar as well as his official actions. Although Holmes and Emerson had usually moved off in different directions from the place where they met, their paths were almost sure to cross again soon. From 1837, when they had both appeared at Harvard's Phi Beta Kappa festivities—Emerson with *The American Scholar* as the oration, Holmes with "A Song of Other Days" as a drinking-song for the dinner—they often were asked to write for or speak at the same occasions. They had served together on Harvard's Board of Overseers during some years in the 1870's, but their most regular meetings were at the Saturday Club, which Emerson had helped to found in 1855, and to which he was as devoted as Holmes. Thus they often followed parallel courses in external events, although from this distance any relation between the two as writers and thinkers would appear chiefly fortuitous.

The biography of Emerson is chiefly notable for Holmes's careful study of Emerson's poems and appreciation of their success in uniting idea and form. Earlier Holmes had been impatient with Emerson's irregularity of line and meter. He still found careless accents and order, but he found much more: with a poet's imagination he brought out the inevitability of phrase and the power of thought. Emerson's prose was more of a chore for him to criticize justly, as he tended to get lost or impatient. But his final impression of the many months of "living in daily relations of intimacy" with Emerson was of "one who seems nearer to me since he left us than while he was here in living form and feature" (VII, 17).[3]

The most memorable tribute Holmes paid to Emerson was in a vein more native to his temperament than biography; it was in the poem he wrote in 1883 which appeared in the *Atlantic* in January, 1884. "At the Saturday Club" (269-71) is in Holmes's familiar couplet, the five-beat rather than the four-beat which he said was the natural rhythm of breathing and which he more often used for comic effect. The longer line here is appropriate to his mood of reminiscence: coming early to the "place of meeting," he falls asleep and remembers in their familiar places those who have died. First is Longfellow, for whom he had written "Our Dead Singer" (271-72), published in the *Atlantic* in June, 1882. After "our Poet Laureate" came the "great Professor"; Holmes's poem "Benjamin Peirce" (143-44) had been in the *Atlantic* for December, 1880, and he had given copies to the ten of the Class of '29 who came to the class dinner in 1881. Agassiz, whose "loss will darken Nature's realm," had been the subject of a poem for his fiftieth birthday in 1857 and of "A Farewell to" (203-4), when he left for his studies in Brazil. "The great Romancer . . . Prouder than Hester, sensitive as Pearl" had been given praise often in prose, but never received a special poem. Holmes reflects a characteristic spontaneity kept intact within the close confines of the couplet and strengthened by the confinement, when he writes at the end, forty lines on Emerson which are the fruit of his long acquaintance and of the study then occupying him. The wide range of analogies is as characteristic of Holmes at his best as the familiar diction which lets him benefit from the couplet's strict form without a resulting rigidity. After noting Emerson as showing "the race-marks of the Brahmin tribe,— / The spare, slight form, the sloping shoulder's droop," he goes into a rush of analogies: "Our Concord Delphi sends its chosen priest"; "the Buddha of the West"; "a wingéd Franklin, sweetly wise, / Born to unlock the secrets of the skies." This play on words he continues without strain or stiffness:

> If lost at times in vague aerial flights,
> None treads with firmer footstep when he lights;
> A soaring nature, ballasted with sense,
> Wisdom without her wrinkles or pretence.

The penetrating comment and apt verses on Emerson here grew, as did the lyric figure of "The Chambered Nautilus," out of concentration on a single person or theme over a period of many months.

III *Poems for Public Occasions*

The range of Holmes's participation by means of poems at public meetings of all sorts may be seen in the table of contents of his collected poems. The headings he chose were: "In Wartime"; "Songs of Welcome and Farewell"; "Memorial Verses"; and "Rhymes of an Hour," the last miscellaneous group including verses written to be sold at fairs for raising money for charitable purposes. The volume of poems *Bunker-Hill Battle and Other Poems* contains in the title the poem he wrote when asked to perform at the centennial celebration in Boston of the Battle of Bunker Hill. "Grandmother's Story of Bunker Hill" (224-27) achieved a place for itself after it appeared on the Memorial Program of the Celebration, June 17, 1875. The woman of eighty who relates what she saw from the belfry makes it intimate and immediate; the sentiment is acceptably warm and familiar when the grandchild is told the wounded soldier's name is "Just your own, my little dear— / There's his picture Copley painted: we became so well acquainted, / That—in short, that's why I'm grandma, / And you children all are here." The anapestic meter Holmes uses has, of course, the stamp of long critical approval for a battle poem; a gleam of wit shines in its being used by a grandmother. It is easy to understand why Whittier, who was often asked for occasional poems but usually refused, judged that the only poet he knew who could move with originality and freshness in the face of an assigned topic was Holmes. The same anapestic meter, but without the warm humor grandma contributed, was used in "Welcome to the Nations" (212), the poem Holmes wrote for the Philadelphia celebration of the hundredth anniversary of the signing of the Declaration of Independence with an International Exhibition on July 4, 1876.

A pronounced interest in libraries and museums becomes apparent as Holmes's occasional publications multiply. He was a vigorous worker for the establishment of the Boston Medical Library, and, as president of the Medical Library Association, he delivered the address at the dedication of the building on December 3, 1878—an address which glows with his own joy in owning and using books, especially works important to medical history. In May, 1883, he went to Philadelphia to prepare with Drs. Gross and Flynt a letter to the American Medical Association to request that an Army Medical Museum and Library be established. So concerned was he about this project that he went to Washington, D.C., December 13-14, 1885, for the first time in forty years to help the cause by personal prestige and spoken appeal. He made the long and painful trip in December to do all in his power to get a National Medical Library started. His earnestness is indicated by the fact that the January before, he had resisted attempts to make him nationally conspicuous by writing for and speaking at the Dedication of the Washington Monument, even though

President A. A. Lawrence of Harvard and the Hon. Robert C. Winthrop had been called on to help persuade Holmes to accept. A serious devotion to preserving treasures of the past could triumph in Holmes over personal vanity.

The anniversary which touched Holmes most personally and helped quiet the gnawing uneasiness about his differing from his father's theological creed, was the two hundred and fiftieth anniversary celebration of his father's former church in Cambridge. The names of three Holmeses appeared on the program: in the afternoon Oliver Wendell Holmes, Jr., gave an address; in the evening the second hymn was "The Word of Promise, (by supposition) An Hymn to be sung by the Great Assembly at Newtown, Mo.12.1.1636. [Written by Oliver Wendell Holmes, eldest son of Rev. Abiel Holmes, eighth Pastor of the First Church]" [*sic*]; the third and last hymn was "Great God, Thou heardst our fathers' prayer, by the Rev. Abiel Holmes, D.D."[4] Oliver Wendell Holmes's hymn characteristically asked for "a common Creed" and that "The Walls that fence his Flocks apart / Shall crack and crumble in Decay." He had tried to rid himself of his persistent theological debate by facing up to the problem in two essays: "Jonathan Edwards" in the *International Review* for July, 1880, and "The Pulpit and the Pew" in the *North American Review* for February, 1881; but it continued to find a place in his informal prose through his last book *Over The Teacups* in 1891.

These two essays were among the few writings of Holmes which were not published by one company in Boston (its name changed from Sampson & Phillips to Ticknor & Fields, to Osgood, and finally, after other changes, to Houghton Mifflin) and by one magazine, the *Atlantic Monthly*, with the exception of strictly professional articles which usually appeared first in the *Boston Medical and Surgical Journal*. This limitation was his own preference: in 1865, he refused to write for George W. Childs's *Harper's Monthly*; in 1866, for Bowen's *Independent;* in 1872, for *Scribner's;* and in 1875, for the *London Athenaeum*. When he retired in 1882, it was announced that henceforth he would devote himself exclusively to writing for the *Atlantic*. But ensuing years showed little change from the pattern of poem, prose article, or a series through the year to be published as a book in November for the Christmas trade, which he had been following with some regularity since the opening number of the *Atlantic* in November, 1857. What did take up his time immediately after his retirement from the Medical School was writing new prefaces and preparing revised editions of his books. He also chose essays to be published in two separate volumes: *Medical Essays 1842-1882* and *Pages From An Old Volume of Life,* which reprinted a few of the essays from the first such collection, *Soundings From the Atlantic* (1864).

Original poems to be publicly presented found the two Wendells consulting together during 1882-83. On January 30, 1883, the doctor read an original poem at the banquet of the Bar Association in Boston, which he had asked his son's advice about before accepting. The December before, his son, now a judge of the Supreme Court of Massachusetts, had asked his father's help on rhymes for a poem he was composing to welcome an English visitor. Wendell and his wife were neighbors on Beacon Street, and lived on familiar terms with the parents at 296, as did Amelia, especially after her husband Turner Sargent died in 1877. The younger son Edward and his wife and son were severely limited in their activities by Edward's increasing ill-health; he died in July, 1884.

IV *A Hundred Days in Europe*

It may have been partly as distraction from this loss and from the daily sorrow of seeing his wife growing weaker in mind and body, as well as to refresh himself from the labor of the Emerson biography and the less arduous but still tiring production of his third novel that Holmes set forth with his daughter Amelia on April 23, 1886, on the journey to England he had long desired. They sailed from Boston to Liverpool on the *Cephalonia,* and Holmes had to sit up nights to ward off painful attacks of asthma. The schedule he and his daughter followed in England would have exhausted a well man, and it is proof of Holmes's resiliency and social genius that he was blithely embarking upon this schedule soon after reaching London. He was unable to attend the festivities planned for him when he landed in Liverpool, but he returned in time to attend a banquet and to respond to a toast on August 20 before he and Amelia sailed for home from that city on August 24 on the *Aurania.*

He was given three British honorary degrees: on June 17, the Doctor of Letters at Cambridge University; on June 25, the

Doctor of Laws at Edinburgh; on June 30, the Doctor of Civil Law at Oxford. The shouts and cheers and calls for a speech from the students on these occasions startled him; at Oxford they asked if he came in the "One-Hoss Shay."[5] The success of *The Autocrat* in England surpassed that of any American book since Irving's *Sketch Book*. *Punch* greeted him with a full-page cartoon by "Spy,"[6] a colored enlargement of which is now in the reading-room of the Boston Medical Library, close by the portrait of Holmes which dominates the room.

Although Holmes had written President Cleveland to persuade him to continue Lowell as ambassador to Great Britain, Holmes's political dabbling had once again been unsuccessful; the new American minister, Edward J. Phelps of Vermont, did all in his power, however, to honor his celebrated compatriot. The two Englishmen who had given the Lowell Institute Lectures in Boston in 1884 and 1885, Edmund Gosse and the Reverend Haweis, were eager hosts, Gosse in Cambridge and Haweis in London. Motley's daughter (Lady Harcourt, wife of the Chancellor of the Exchequer) introduced her father's friend and biographer to her friends in high places. Holmes visited Tennyson at the Isle of Wight through the offices of Tennyson's son-in-law Frederick Locker-Lampson. He went to the Derby, this time in the Prince of Wales's private car; and he was fêted in London by the Literary Society as well as by the Rabelais Club to which he had been elected in 1880. Browning, whom he met at many affairs, impressed him with his energy and robustness.

But as he told his friendly readers of *Our Hundred Days in Europe,* the trip was chiefly a personal social triumph—as well as a severe test of physical endurance. His daughter Amelia proved as resourceful and helpful as her mother, keeping the engagements straight and protecting her father, a man of seventy-seven plagued by asthma and susceptible to colds, without interfering too much with his predilections. The response to England of the Autocrat and the Poet Laureate of Boston in 1886 was the opposite of the slightly negative reaction of the medical student of 1834-35: England, especially London, was now a Mecca for the man of letters famous for his witty talk and quick, flattering response. Holmes's appetite for personal conspicuousness and attentive, admiring audiences had been whetted by success and repeated invitations; without the duties of his medical position

and with loneliness and sorrow entering the home where he had
found strength and a balance for his egotism through long
years, he turned with alacrity to the role of honored guest, where
pleasure and diversion were as sure as ever.

Holmes and his daughter returned to a Boston made sad for
both because Mrs. Holmes's health and memory continued to fail.
What more natural than that Holmes should find happiness in
writing a public bread-and-butter letter to his recent hosts, for
himself and for his fellow-Americans? The *Atlantic* columns were
as open to him under Thomas Bailey Aldrich as they had been
under Lowell and Howells. Although the friendly publisher James
T. Fields had died in April, 1881, his death brought no change
in editorial policy that would affect Holmes's close relations
with the magazine. So from January to December, 1887, *Our
Hundred Days in Europe* set down the honors the public image
of the Autocrat had enjoyed in England, and it included enough
about his physical sufferings to explain to the English and the
Americans why he was becoming so neglectful of his personal
correspondents. A printed folder was prepared for him in
November, 1887, probably by Amelia Sargent and Fanny Holmes,
who were close enough to realize the burden imposed by piles
of incoming letters on one who insisted on writing personal
replies to all. The printed folder explained that "impaired
eyesight" made it impossible for Holmes to give his correspondents the attention they had come to expect; but he rarely
sent the folder without a personal note on the leaf inside, or
a note dictated to his secretary and signed by himself. Personal
idiosyncrasies tend to become more accented as the years mount,
and it was useless for Amelia Sargent and Fanny Holmes to try
to change the habits of the author who was blamed by fellow
authors for being so generous with his response to requests for
autographs that they were forced to follow his example or be
reproached with it.

Our Hundred Days gave Holmes the chance, through the
pages of the *Atlantic* or of the book, which appeared both in
Boston and London in September, 1887, to express his pleasure
and gratitude to his friendly hosts in Great Britain, and to let
other Americans share in the warm good-will. The wide sales the
book enjoyed, the best since *The Guardian Angel* in 1867, gave
evidence that readers in the United States and in England accepted the book as he had intended.

CHAPTER 6

A Pleasant or a Tedious Afterpiece?

IN HIS Harvard Phi Beta Kappa oration of 1871, *Mechanism in Thought and Morals,* Holmes warned that every new generation should be heeded because "Civilized as well as savage races live upon their parents and grandparents," and he concluded with a figure of life as a play: "The prologue of life is finished here at twenty: then come five acts of a decade each, and the play is over, with now and then a pleasant or a tedious afterpiece, when half the lights are put out, and half the orchestra is gone" (99). Two lights were put out for Holmes in February, 1888, when his wife and James Freeman Clarke died—the latter had been his classmate, pastor, and close friend during sixty years. The death of his wife was the finality of physical loss, as for ten years she had not been able physically or mentally to fulfill her role of practical and ideal helpmeet. But daughter Amelia sold her house, and came to live at 296 Beacon Street with Holmes. The shadow in Holmes's personal life grew really dark when she became ill early in 1889 and died in April. No wonder he took to writing the last stanza of "The Last Leaf" in books he inscribed and for fairs for which he continued to supply autographs. He had started to resurrect the Breakfast-Table essays by the device of people who gathered to exchange ideas or papers or poems, or to listen to the Professor or the Dictator; now it had appropriately become a Tea-Table, and the people were called Teacups, all sound and normal save Number Seven, the cracked Teacup with "the squinting brain."

I *The Dictator*

This series had started in the *Atlantic* for March, 1888, but Amelia's death and the change when young Wendell and his wife Fanny came to run the house at 296 Beacon Street kept

Holmes from resuming the articles until July, 1890, when they continued through November. Even with many of the old figures present and the old ideas to touch again with a few new ones, the vein ran out before the year was completed. The last numbers make clear why wise friends advised him to stop even though the old man enjoyed sitting down with pen and paper and writing himself back to happier days. Too obviously he was reliving the days of the Autocrat—now called the Dictator, for Holmes knew better than to revive that popular figure. Cherished memories were resurrected, but the effects were chiefly repetitious. Some freshness and topical value came with the story of the maid called Delilah. After five weeks of serving at the Tea-Table, she disappeared. This caused some suspicious-looking absences of the young Doctor. When the teacups embarked upon a journey to a neighboring college for young women to attend the Exhibition at Commencement, the gold medal was accepted by Delilah, whose real name proved to be Avis. She had been forced by ill health to take a change of work and environment for five weeks, and she had then won the hearts at the Tea-Table. Here Holmes was using his experience of being an honorary member of the Class of 1887 at Wellesley: on December 8, 1884, he had visited the college, been welcomed by President Alice Freeman (not yet married to Harvard Professor George Palmer), but had spent most of the day with the Class, reading them "Dorothy Q.," "Bill and Joe," and "The Boys"—making it "a red-letter day in the annals of 1887."[1]

Another autobiographical echo is the poem about Bar Harbor, "La Maison D'Or" (IV, 172; 301). The title of the poem is a shameless pun on the name of his hostess, Mrs. Julia Dorr, whom Amelia had taken him to visit for a few days in the summer of 1888. Mrs. Dorr was the Vermont poetess with whom Holmes had long corresponded; now a widow, she spent her winters in Boston and her summers in Bar Harbor, the newly chosen playground of the wealthy. From his own experience of "The restful mountains and the restless sea" Holmes could draw his two-stanza picture and lesson. Poems at the Tea-Table were only occasionally identified by author: usually they were found in the sugar-bowl or the urn on the table.

Besides the topical reference to a recent cultural growth, the "college for young women," Holmes laughed at the new labor organizations. Two of the foreign-born, Mike Fagan and Hans Schleimer, were pitted against Hiram, the native New Hampshireman who worked for the "Mistress" of the boarding-house. Hiram finally used his shovel to get rid of these impertinent fellows who wanted to know how much he was paid and how many hours a day he worked. Irish and German dialects were used to make ridiculous the proud title of "Knights of Labor." The irony of laborers' and American fondness for such high-sounding titles took him off on this subject which he had glanced at in *The Poet;* he developed the early extreme example of Lord Timothy Dexter of Newburyport (IV, 232-33), an eccentric whom the late John P. Marquand also enjoyed exhuming.

More serious was his comment on social prejudice. Like *Our Hundred Days, Over the Teacups* became a means of writing public letters, especially when Holmes wanted to correct or explain. At some length he corrected a statement purported to be his and so quoted in the *Journal of the American Medical Association* (April 29, 1890): ". . . give me opium, wine, and milk, and I will cure all diseases to which flesh is heir" (IV, 189-90). In *The American Hebrew* (April 4, 1890) four questions had been asked about the causes of prejudice against Jews in American society, and Holmes took them up with the same tolerance he had expressed most often for all sects of Protestantism, and occasionally for Roman Catholicism. The stately synagogue had its place beside the aspiring cathedral because "there are many mansions in the Father's earthly house as well as in the heavenly one." Most moving are the four stanzas from his earlier poem "At the Pantomime" (189); the poem had been written in 1859, and published then in a Hebrew collection in New York; it was rewritten in 1874; in 1890 it was used again. The author tells of being crowded in between two Israelites on a hot afternoon at the pantomime; as the poet reviles the Jews, using the darkest invective against them as usurers and murderers of Christians, he looks more closely at one neighbor and sees the resemblance to "The Maiden's Boy of Bethlehem." Only the last four stanzas are used here, which conclude " 'Peace be upon thee, Israel!' " (IV, 193-99).

Although the last poem included in this series of articles is called "Invita Minerva" and accepts the truth that the Muse "will not hear thy call" and it is better to "await no more / The rush of heaven-sent wings" (IV, 314; 305), at least one poem shows the old originality and freshness which could transmute the familiar by imaginative analogy—and often with an incongruity which amuses while it liberates. This poem is read by Number Five, he of "the squinting brain," whose sallies often bring home to those assembled that it is "the cranks that make the wheels in all the world go round" (IV, 161), or that "a slight mental obliquity" is to be found in most mortals (IV, 282). In this poem the new trolley-cars take him back to the days of the Salem witches, and the gay four-beat couplets of "The Broomstick Train; or, The Return of the Witches" (IV, 226-30; 301-4) were widely recited and enjoyed—until trolley-cars became as obsolete as witches. An echo of an old argument may be heard in the Professor's ridicule of specialists in medicine and the defense of them by the young Doctor. Holmes's being called "A Moral Parricide" in an attack in a church paper when the opposition to Calvinistic orthodoxy in *The Professor* was still rankling, is referred to here and thoroughly argued down by summarizing points made in the essays "Jonathan Edwards" and "The Pulpit and the Pew."

The question of admitting women to medical studies is given the same affirmative answer as in real life and in *A Mortal Antipathy,* when one of the two Annexes expresses her wish to be a doctor (IV, 131). The Annexes are two young girls, one English and one American; the English girl is rounded off by her manner of speech when she remarks " 'Fancy! how very-very odd!' " Holmes's eyesight might be impaired, but there was nothing wrong with his ears during his travels in England. Like most of the figures who appear in this last book, the Annexes come to life only occasionally; the Teacups have even less reality than the group at the Poet's Breakfast-Table. After initial intimate comments which identify people and places, Holmes spends some time warning his readers that the Teacups are not to be identified, except as we meet old friends like the Professor. The Tutor and the Counsellor are interesting chiefly in their relation to Number Five, the gracious lady whom all love but who remains aloof at the same time that she is always ready with the appropriate word or gesture. One is tempted to infer that his son and daughter-in-law wanted him to have the consolation of being busy with his pen as in the old days, but did issue warnings against his using details that were readily identifiable.

Number Five is the most idealized woman Holmes ever

created: it is as if he were re-creating tenderly the various schoolmistresses and the wife whose memory became more precious every year. His longing for the special kind of feminine companionship the latter had given him is suggested by his turning to several women at this time with a candid longing for tenderness that had never appeared before. Annie Fields, who had continued to live on terms of intimacy with the Holmeses in Boston after the death of her husband, was called on most often when he was lonely, and his many brief notes to her at this time reveal how lost he sometimes felt—a mood never allowed to appear in the public image. Although old age is often mentioned, and the figure of the vessel which started with a full crew and is now reduced to a "raft where I cling" appears and reappears after 1890, the final word must always be hopeful. Thus his poem on those no longer present "At the Saturday Club" closes: "Yet life is lovelier for these transient gleams / Of buried friendships; blest is he who dreams!"

Other women besides Annie Fields were glad to bring him flowers and take him to drive. Mrs. Dorr came often when she was back from Bar Harbor. Another authoress-correspondent of many years' standing, Elizabeth Stuart Phelps, had married Herbert D. Ward in October, 1888, but she was near enough on Cape Ann in summer to drive over often, and she wrote him just as regularly as ever during the winter. He always had two tickets for the season of the Boston Symphony, and he escorted a lady to the concerts; though, when he fell asleep during one in November, 1890, he almost decided he should not venture forth again, so acute was his embarrassment. But he continued, and, in January, 1891, he heard perform and met Mrs. Helen Hopekirk Wilson, a concert pianist. She was charmed to be sought out by the famous author, and for a year or two they corresponded with intimacy. This correspondence is the clearest indication of the old man's seeking distraction in new acquaintances; of his pathetically eager desire to prove to himself and others that he was not being made much of just because he was an old friend who had to be coddled, or because he was so old that people were surprised and curious to discover that he was still alive. He had joked about this kind of fame at eighty; at eighty-three the objective view that made for comedy came more rarely even to this man whose "automatic mind" must have had well-worn tracks in that direction.

II *Memorials and Honors*

Holmes was still apt and tender in the memorial poems or prose tributes he continued to write as more of his beloved companions died. His poem "James Russell Lowell" (296-97) began with utter sincerity "Thou shouldst have sung the swan-song for the choir / That filled our groves with music." Although the poem for Whittier in the *Atlantic* for November, 1892 (297), is equally sincere, his prose tribute in a letter read at the Whittier Commemoration of the Young Men's Christian Union, October 16, 1892, is more movingly eloquent; tender memory has enriched this prose and sharpened the picture. His tribute to George William Curtis for the memorial meeting of the Unitarian Club of New York in November, 1892, shows that Holmes could praise a faith he shared as variously and persuasively as he attacked a creed that made him shudder: "the faith which has shaken off the last rusty links of the chains forged in the ages of civil and religious despotism." That Curtis was a Unitarian and Whittier a Quaker made not a whit of difference to Holmes; that both had preached a "gospel of humanity" was what counted.

Holmes's last recorded public appearance was at a reception given by publishers to the members of the National Education Association in Boston, February 23, 1893, where he was one of several authors presented. His prefatory remarks as well as his poem "To the Teachers of America" (298) were printed and reprinted. He had not known until ten-thirty that morning that anything more than an appearance and words of greeting would be expected of him. The "automatic mind" must have behaved in exemplary fashion that morning because the poem he read after he arrived at one-thirty in the afternoon was smooth, rapid, brightened by rhyme and figure—by no means vapid with trite phrases. His poem on "Francis Parkman" was later (November 21, 1893) and appeared in the *Atlantic* in February, 1894, only eight months before his own death. But it was read by Holmes at the memorial meeting of the Massachusetts Historical Society, and the meeting of a society which has consistently been as notable and exclusive as that group could scarcely be termed "public."

In the ten years after Holmes retired from the Harvard Medical School in 1882, he was honored by members of the medical profession in three cities. A banquet was arranged by the medical profession of New York City at Delmonico's on April 12, 1883. This group went to the trouble of designing the invitations as a telegram showing Holmes hurrying along with a bundle of books under one arm and a bundle of bones under the other and pursued by a policeman with a sign reading "Tewkesbury Investigation." The reference was to Governor Ben Butler and his political investigation of the use of bodies from Massachusetts charitable institutions for dissection; naturally Holmes had been called to testify at the hearings. At this New York banquet, Holmes, according to reports, was as witty and entertaining as the invitation by cartoon invited him to be. In London in 1886, he had been honored at a dinner by the medical profession, and gave evidence of what *Punch* said of him in a poem after his death: "Finished scholar, poet, wit . . . Age chilled not your fire of fun" (Morse, II, 97). But on April 30, 1892, he was unable to receive in person a third formal tribute arranged in Philadelphia by his fellow novelist-physician Dr. S. Weir Mitchell. The latter had had Holmes's portrait painted by Mrs. Sarah Whitman, however reluctant may have been the subject, who had always considered "his face a convenience rather than an ornament." The formal presentation to the Philadelphia College of Physicians was made with only the portrait and a grateful letter representing Holmes.

It is unfortunate that so much publicity has been given to scraps of conversation or anecdote chiefly pertinent to the last five years of the doctor's life, when he was relying more than he ever had before on the flattery of calls and gifts—was clinging pathetically to the image he had created through the years. His passion for being known and praised was uncomfortable to the son busy with his close study of the law, his speeches, his writings on *The Common Law*—as it would have been foreign to the medical student working on his study of puerperal fever in 1843. That the father was more prying and more insistent on his own rules for public speaking and writing than would be acceptable to a young man of brilliant intellect and originality is probable. While Mrs. Holmes had been alive and active, she had kept the public image that the father increasingly displayed and delighted in safely shut off in the upstairs library, out of disturbing articulation in the family circle. She recognized that the sensitive affection between the two Wendells was often strained by the elder's too facile intrusions, and she could impose a restraint that mollified the younger and kept a balance between two personalities whose gifts differed as startlingly as they sometimes showed resemblances.

The younger Holmes compared the burden of fixed ideas and accepted rules of action on the law to similar encumbrances on theology—just as his father had linked medicine with theology when he fought for emancipation from traditional medical practices not tested by experiment. The son called "revolting" the fact that a law could exist for no other reason than that it had existed in the past; it was more revolting when investigation proved the original grounds for the law had disappeared. All three generations of Holmeses set a high value on history: Abiel Holmes's real claim to remembrance lay in his careful recording in *Annals of America;* his son eloquently reminded medical men of the need for libraries to preserve the contributions of great thinkers of the past (he gave his own medical books to the Boston Medical Library in June, 1889), at the same time that he called for constant testing of all traditional theories in the light of advances and discoveries; the grandson wrote "A page of history is worth a volume of logic," but he added "the present has a right to govern itself so far as it can; and it ought always to be remembered that historic continuity with the past is not a duty, it is only a necessity."[2] The persistently comic attitude of the elder Wendell became a darker irony in the younger, for his skepticism went deeper than the questioning of established man-made creeds and laws. The twentieth-century search for a rational pattern in the universe, that has forced many back toward the darker doctrines of the Puritans to explain such contemporary outrages of "the brotherhood of man" as cruel oppressions and senseless massacres, was reflected in the son who lived until 1935; the emphasis on social progress and increasing hope for the welfare of humanity in the elder Holmes was as characteristic of the intellectual climate of the nineteenth century. Both elder and younger would join in the elder's expressed relief at the change he had lived to see: "In the more intelligent circles of American society one may question anything and everything, if he will only do it civilly" (IV, 251). The nineteenth-century Holmes was enough of a practical observer to qualify his announcement by "more intelligent"; the Scopes trial was still possible in Tennessee in the 1920's.

When Oliver Wendell Holmes died on October 7, 1894, President Eliot of Harvard sent out the formal notice on note-paper edged in black:

> It is with great regret that I inform you of the death of Oliver Wendell Holmes, Professor of Anatomy, *Emeritus,* which occurred on the 7th instant in the eighty-sixth year of his age.
>
> The funeral services will be held at King's Chapel, Boston, on Wednesday, October 10, at noon.[3]

It rained at noon on October 10, but classmates May and Smith went to the funeral together. May had received a note from the living Wendell: "Knowing my father's affection for you I should have written you earlier had I known your address. His death was as peaceful as one could wish for those one loves. He simply ceased to breathe. The funeral will be held at King's Chapel on Wednesday at 12. I have asked that a pew should be kept in case one or two classmates should feel able to come."[4]

The inscription on the memorial tablet to Holmes in King's Chapel, Boston, was provided by President Eliot, and it celebrates the success Holmes attained during his lifetime in several fields: original research in medicine; a mastery of familiar verse, which Dr. Johnson had perceptively noted was the most difficult and the least often mastered; and the creation of an original form in the prose of his Breakfast-Table series. As Holmes clearly saw and often wrote, concentration on a single issue is more likely to bring immortality than a wide-ranging facility. He was surely overvalued in his own day; he suffered a correspondingly greater fall from favor with critics of the succeeding generation. But with the advent of scientific fiction, readers find his novels more interesting for being "medicated." His place in American medical history was attained early and has remained secure. His writings still offer the surprise of analogy and the imaginative range of figure; both often combine amusing incongruity with picturesque clarity. Perhaps the pleasure his readers enjoy most often is the pleasure of recognition of "What oft was thought, but ne'er so well expressed." The inscription on the tablet in memory of Oliver Wendell Holmes in King's Chapel closes appropriately with an appreciation of his successful mingling of the useful with the pleasant: the Latin phrase from Horace's *Ars Poetica,* "Miscuit Utile Dulci."

Notes and References

Chapter One

1. *The Complete Poetical Works of Oliver Wendell Holmes*, ed. Horace E. Scudder, Cambridge ed. (Boston [1908]), pp. 186-87. References in the text by page in Arabic numeral are to this volume.

Biographical material is scattered through *Life and Letters of Oliver Wendell Holmes* by John Torrey Morse, Jr. (Boston, 1896). Morse was the nephew of Mrs. Holmes, and had access to MSS and records which have since disappeared, if they cannot be found in the Library of Harvard University or the Library of Congress. Morse printed many Holmes letters, but with omissions or changes not indicated; hence I give the reference to Morse, but quote from the original where it is available.

Only in Morse may be found what he said was Holmes's start on an autobiography, his "Autobiographical Notes," I, [28]-51.

2. Henry Chandler Bowen, owner of the *Independent* and the *Brooklyn Union*, had won wide notice through the opposition to slavery and the vigorous support of worthy causes in the papers he controlled.

3. Morse, I, 16. The passage quoted is from part of a letter to Holmes in 1868 from Col. T. W. Higginson, who had found the reference in a girlhood letter written by his mother, and had copied out the part about Abiel Holmes for the son.

4. a.l.s. Holmes to Mary [Parsons], Cambridge, September 29, 1822. In Houghton Library, Harvard, and used here with the permission of the Director, William A. Jackson.

5. Upham had been a brilliant student in the class of 1821 at Harvard and had studied at the Cambridge Divinity School before he became pastor of the First Unitarian Church in Salem, where he and Ann lived until his death in 1875 and hers in 1877. He and Holmes were alike in preferring a liberal and rational Christianity to the rigid Calvinistic doctrine. Upham had a political career also. He served in the House and Senate of the Massachusetts Legislature and as Member of Congress from 1853 to 1855.

His political influence has made him a candidate for the original of Judge Pyncheon, the satiric portrait in Hawthorne's *The House of the Seven Gables*. Evidence does point to his being, as Hawthorne believed, one of those who caused Hawthorne's removal from the post of Collector of Customs at the Port of Salem. Upham is best known today for his two-volume study of *Salem Witchcraft* (Boston,

1867). Hearing so much about witches in his sister's house in Salem helped Holmes to sketch in colorfully the details of his last amusing poetic analogy. In 1890, the new trolley-car became "The Broomstick Train; Or, The Return of the Witches" (pp. 301-4).

6. *North American Review,* XCIX (April, 1838), 481.

7. From a.l.s. Holmes to the Rev. William Jenks, Boston, February 21, 1838. This letter is in the Henry W. and Albert A. Berg Collection of the New York Public Library; it is quoted from here and on p. 33 with the permission of the Business Manager, George L. Schaefer.

8. *The Writings of Oliver Wendell Holmes.* Riverside ed. (Boston, 1891), III, 28. Quotations from Holmes's prose are from this edition unless otherwise noted. References are usually in the text by Roman and Arabic numerals. This edition is described in the bibliography.

9. *Letters of John Holmes to James Russell Lowell and Others,* ed. William Roscoe Thayer (Boston, 1917), p. 63. Introduction by Alice M. Longfellow, pp. [xi]-xlvii.

10. Miriam R. Small, "First and Last Surviving Poems of Dr. Oliver Wendell Holmes," *American Literature,* XV (January, 1944), 416-17. The last poem was four lines in French written in the front of Vol. I of his *Poetical Works* (Edinburgh, 1892), for the actress Ellen Terry:

> Ellen Terry
> Sur la scène
> Toujours La Reine;
> Sans diademe
> Encore la même.

> Hommage d[e] l'Auteur.
> Oliver Wendell Holmes
> Boston, Jan. 17th 1894.

The old man of eighty-four was gallantly returning to the French of his student days when he first saw great acting in Paris; in this poem he shows skill with the short line in French. The volume containing Holmes's inscription was found and given to me by Professor Emeritus Chauncey Brewster Tinker of Yale University.

11. These quotations are from two letters from Holmes to "Lyddy" Murdock, later Mrs. N. S. Richardson of Bridgeport, Conn.: June 10, 1893, and June 19, 1894. I owe these letters and permission to quote from them to Mrs. Dunbar Hunt Ogden of New Orleans, grandniece of Mrs. Richardson.

12. The signed autograph lines, framed, are preserved in the Maine Historical Society, Portland. In 1924, they were given to the Society with an explanatory note by Dr. Charles Sias Wright of the U.S.

Marine Hospital at Woodford's Junction. Ann was his grandmother and she had kept and framed the verses; she named her son Abiel Holmes Wright—prophetically, since he became a well-known clergyman in Portland. The lines are used here with the permission of the Maine Historical Society.

13. For a detailed account of the exchanges on both sides of the parish quarrel, see Eleanor M. Tilton, *Amiable Autocrat* (New York, 1947), pp. 43-49; 56-58.

14. From a.l.s. Holmes to the Rev. William Jenks, Boston, February 21, 1838. See note 7.

15. Franklin T. Currier, ed. Eleanor M. Tilton, *Bibliography of Oliver Wendell Holmes* (New York, 1953), pp. 333, 207. Hereafter this will be noted as *Bibliog.*, and special attention called only when my information supplements or differs from the full information there on all matters relating to editions, issues, and identification.

16. Tilton, p. 71. For a study of medical practices and teachers Holmes encountered in Boston and Paris, see chapters five through ten, pp. 69-176.

17. The letters Holmes wrote from abroad to his mother and father, to his brother John, to his brothers-in-law the Rev. Charles Upham in Salem and Dr. Parsons in Providence, were carefully preserved, sumptuously bound, and are now in the Harvard Holmes Collection in Houghton Library. Morse used these letters for his biography, but often omitted names and revealing comments which today constitute their chief interest. His omissions from this body of letters are the urgent pleas for money to travel and to continue his study abroad, which are appealing in their youthful desperation and amusing in their attempts to persuade his elders of opportunities he cannot afford to miss.

18. In the *Bibliothèque de l'École de Médecine* in Paris, I have seen the records of this period which were not destroyed by fire during the siege of Paris in 1870. The only place Holmes's name appears is in the records of attendance of "Séances de la Société médicale d'emulation." The French word *emulation* suggests the competitive nature of the group more than the English word *Observation*. Holmes signed as *étranger* nine times from Dec. 7, 1833 to April 19, 1834. As one of the *membres titulaires* he was absent only three times from Sept. 22, 1834 through July 8, 1835. The last meeting he attended was on Oct. 17, 1835, before he sailed for home. Although he wrote his friend John Sargent that he had prepared "thirty thick-set pages" for the Society, his name does not appear in the list of *Procès-verbaux* (1834-1837).

19. Morse, I, 130, but form of a.l.s. in Houghton Library, Harvard, is followed here with the permission of the Director, William A. Jackson.

Chapter Two

1. *Bolyston Prize Dissertations for the Years 1836-7* (Boston, 1838), p. 17. Holmes brought out his three Prize Essays together, with a dedication to Louis "in the Recollection of His Invaluable Instructions and Unvarying Kindness." See *Bibliog.*, pp. 28-29.

2. Dr. Edwin H. Ackerknecht, "Malaria in the Upper Mississippi Valley," *Bulletin of the History of Medicine*, Supplement No. 4 (Baltimore, 1945), p. 55.

3. John O. Sargent must have been after Holmes for verses again, because three parts of this poem appeared with separate titles in *Sargent's New Monthly Magazine* for January, February, and March, 1843. It was first published as a whole in 1940: *At Dartmouth*, with an introduction by Eleanor M. Tilton (N.Y., 1940). See *Bibliog.*, pp. 263-64.

4. The second Edward Jackson Holmes died childless in 1945 and the line was extinct. The Holmes house at 296 Beacon Street had been sold earlier, and many manuscripts and books were given to form part of the Harvard Holmes Collection. Most of the manuscripts and books which Justice Holmes had taken to Washington were left to the Library of Congress upon his death. The Holmes house is still standing, and back of it on Embankment Road is a sundial with an inscription noting Holmes's residence here by the Charles River. Unfortunately the recent Storrow Drive has made noisy and noisome the pleasant walk by the river with its flavor of comfortable nineteenth-century brownstone backs.

5. As recently as 1937, I met a doctor who was still fighting Holmes's views on homeopathy as set forth in *Homœopathy and Its Kindred Delusions*. The Society for the Diffusion of Useful Knowledge had published his second and third lectures under this title in April, 1842; under Holmes's supervision it was republished three times—in 1861, 1883, and 1891. The twentieth-century doctor concluded his bitter attack on Holmes's medical thinking as blind and hopelessly prejudiced by mentioning that he was a homeopath himself. When I found out through a medical dictionary that he was the president of an existing Institute of Homeopathy, I understood why his attitude toward Holmes differed so sharply from the respect I had met in doctors who collected early printings of Holmes's works as a significant part of American medical history.

6. Dr. Henry R. Viets in *The Bulletin of the Medical Library Association* (October, 1943).

7. *Boston Medical and Surgical Journal*, LIV (Feb. 28, 1856), 81. At the time Holmes was carrying on his most dedicated crusade in behalf of the helpless mothers in this country, Ignatz Philipp

Semmelweiss was fighting the same battle against entrenched doctors in the Lying-In Hospital in Vienna. For a while he succeeded in saving lives by isolating patients from infection-carrying doctors; but he was shortly ousted by authorities, returned to Budapest, and died in an insane asylum, a martyr to his cause. As time proved him right, he was honored by a monument in Budapest; and in his native city of Eisenstadt in Burgenland (then in Hungary, now in Austria), his birthplace is maintained as a museum in honor of the European investigator who proved infection was the cause of epidemics of puerperal fever.

8. Holmes's most important professional essay was reprinted recently in *Medical Classics*, compiled by Emerson Crosby Kelly, M.D., I (Baltimore, November, 1936), [195]-268.

9. Edward Warren, *Some Account of the Letheon* (2nd ed.; Boston, 1847), p. 79. The first edition was hastily arranged and did not carry Holmes's letter, but it was the final item in the second and third editions. During the controversy with three other claimants to the discovery—Charles Jackson of Boston, Horace Wells of Hartford, and Dr. Crawford Long of Georgia—Holmes performed only one act for Morton. He wrote his New Orleans classmate Isaac Morse, who was a member of Congress when Morton's claim was being argued, pointing out that Morton was the only one who had succeeded in having test operations performed whereby his discovery was authenticated.

10. Letter to Griswold, Sept. 1, 1843, in George B. Ives, *Bibliography of Oliver Wendell Holmes* (Boston, 1907), p. 77. This earlier bibliography is valuable for giving Dr. Holmes's contributions to the *Atlantic Monthly* chronologically by volume. This list is in my bibliography because Ives's is not easily available and because these contributions show the variety of Holmes's literary activities from 1857 to 1894. To avoid duplication, references to the *Atlantic* in text and notes are only by month and year.

11. Because "The Pilgrim's Vision" referred to two wars with England, it was kept out of the London edition of 1846; it appeared first in the Boston edition of 1849.

12. a.l.s. Holmes to [Fields], Dec. 29, 1846. In the Henry W. and Albert A. Berg Collection of the New York Public Library, and used here with the permission of the Business Manager, George L. Schaefer.

13. a.l.s. Holmes to Griswold, April 27, 1842. In the Simon Gratz Collection of the Pennsylvania Historical Society; used here with the permission of the Director, R. N. Williams II.

Almost fifty years later, in December, 1891, in a letter to Whittier (Morse, 11, 316), Holmes's figure was different: "I have just been

looking over the headstones in Mr. Griswold's cemetery entitled
The Poets and Poetry of America."

14. a.l.s. Holmes to Emerson, Jan. 14, 1847. In Houghton Library,
Harvard; used here with the permission of the Director, William A.
Jackson.

15. *Ms.s* in Massachusetts Historical Society, Miscellaneous; used
here with the permission of the Director, Stephen T. Riley.

16. *Letters of John Holmes . . .* , p. 14.

17. This letter has been printed many times, but the reading
here is from the a.l.s. in Houghton Library, Harvard, with permission
of Director William A. Jackson.

18. For contemporary references to the shower that forced the
host and his guests to run for cover on Monument Mountain, see
Tilton, pp. 220-22.

19. For detail of subjects and itineraries of lyceum lectures, of
dates and reception of the Lowell Institute Lectures, see *Bibliog.*,
Appendix 5, pp. 526-36.

20. "A Visit to the Autocrat's Landlady" in *Soundings From the
Atlantic* (Boston, 1864), p. 337. The essay first appeared in the
Atlantic for November, 1858, as "By the Special Reporter of the
Oceanic Miscellany."

21. From a.l.s. Motley to Holmes, Nov. 20, 1853. In the Houghton
Library, Harvard; used here by permission of Director William A.
Jackson.

22. *Essays and Reviews* (New York, 1848), I, 64-65. The comment is from an essay-review of Griswold's *Poets and Poetry of
America*, originally the leading article in *North American Review*,
LVIII (January, 1844), 1-39. Holmes's a.l.s. to Whipple, Jan. 8,
1849, is privately owned.

23. A volume of *Songs and Poems of '29* was privately printed
for the class in 1852, 1859, 1868, and 1881. Three copies in 1881
were especially bound for the three most honored singers: Holmes,
Samuel F. Smith, and the Rev. James Freeman Clarke. A later
volume, *Latest Poems 1882-1889*, carried few poems except those
by Holmes.

24. These a.l.s. Holmes to President Eliot are in the Harvard
Archives; they are quoted from here with the permission of Custodian
Clifford K. Shipton.

25. Besides these lectures which kept Holmes before the public
during the war years, a new volume of poems, *Songs in Many Keys*,
appeared in 1861, besides two editions of his *Poems*: the Blue and
Gold in 1862; and the Cabinet in 1863. Both contained the war
poems through 1861. The *Poems* of Longfellow, Whittier, and Lowell
preceded Holmes's in the Blue and Gold edition.

26. *Bibliog.*, pp. 126-27, reports the first delivery of the lecture "Poetry of the War" to have been in Cambridge in November, 1865, but a.l.s. Holmes to Lowell, Dec. 16, 1865, makes clear it was given in New York first, and repeated in shortened form. The a.l.s. is in Houghton Library, Harvard; it is referred to here with the permission of Director William A. Jackson.

27. "Class Poems of '29" were first set in a separate section, as were also poems "In Wartime," "Songs of Welcome and Farewell," and "Memorial Verses," in *Songs of Many Seasons 1862-1874*, published in 1875. These sections were kept, and all but the poems "In Wartime" added to, in the Household edition of Holmes's *Poetical Works* in 1877, which was issued as an Illustrated Library edition in 1885, and as the *Complete Poetical Works* in 1887.

28. *Proceedings of the Harvard Club of New York City*, Feb. 21, 1878, pp. 16-17.

29. The Handy Volume edition in two volumes of Holmes's *Poetical Works* appeared in 1881; but if it was intended to implement the farewell in "The Iron Gate," it didn't work out that way. Because in 1888, another volume appeared, *Before the Curfew*. This appeared in an English edition the same year, perhaps because the English could not forget their popular visitor of 1886, and were eager for more of his poems. This proved to be the last volume of new poems, but the poems were part of the collected editions of his *Writings* which came out during his last years under his supervision: the Riverside edition, 1891; the Standard Library, 1892; the Illustrated Standard, called the Artists' edition, 1893.

30. a.l.s. Holmes to President Eliot, Dec. 11, 1888. This letter has been printed often, but the reading here is from the autograph in the Harvard Archives, with the permission of Custodian Clifford K. Shipton.

Chapter Three

1. Although this a.l.s. was marked "Private" at the top of the first leaf, it was printed in facsimile in Higginson and Boynton, *A Reader's History of American Literature* (Boston [1903]), facing p. 158. The reading here is from the autograph owned by the late discriminating collector-scholar Carroll A. Wilson, and called by him the finest Holmes letter he owned.

2. a.l.s. Holmes to Miss Charlotte Dana, April 18, 1863, in the Massachusetts Historical Society, Dana Papers; used here with the permission of Director Stephen T. Riley.

3. Osler's first reference to this question was in the "Notes and Commentaries" he had been writing for the *Montreal Medical Journal* (January, 1889). Holmes's reply was written on Jan. 21, 1889, and

was twice printed by Osler. The original letter is now in the collection of Osleriana in the McGill Medical Library in Montreal. For a full account of Osler's regard for Holmes, see Harvey Cushing, *Life of Sir William Osler* (Oxford, 1926), I, 301-2.

4. Four editions of *The Autocrat* appeared in this country before the new and revised edition in 1883; five issues of it came before Holmes's death in 1894, five after. Modern reprints have appeared in Oxford's World's Classics in 1904 (reprinted 1906, 1909, 1923, then allowed to lapse); in Macmillan's Modern Readers' series in 1927; and in the New American Library of World Literature's Signet Classics in 1961.

Both the first and the revised editions appeared promptly in Edinburgh: the first, 1859; the revised, 1883. Although there were only two English editions—one in 1859, and an illustrated edition in 1865—*The Autocrat* won an enthusiastic audience there, as a result of which Holmes's distaste for that country began to give way to an eager desire to visit it again, especially after his friends Lowell and Motley were writing him of English experiences he could wish to share. A German translation came out in Stuttgart in 1876, *Der Tisch-Despot;* in Leipzig, a Tauchnitz edition in 1883. In 1922, it was published in Japan as one of the Kenkyusha English Classics.

Besides these single printings, it was Volume I in the collected editions of 1891, 1892, and 1893.

5. This scrapbook is now in the Oliver Wendell Holmes Library of Phillips-Andover Academy.

6. I omit *American* here intentionally. In 1933, when I attended at the Crystal Palace in London a service of song presided over by the Archbishop of Canterbury and performed by the different cathedral choirs of England in their robes of varying colors and with their choir-masters and organists, this hymn by Holmes was chosen to close the program.

7. That *The Professor* by no means matched *The Autocrat* in popularity is shown by a brief review of the printings. Under the title *The Story of Iris,* the parts concerning her were published separately in 1877; a reprint of this, with a section of *Favorite Poems* by Holmes and another section of five sermons by Dr. John Brown was issued in the Modern Classics, No. 30, in 1882. A revised edition, to match that of *The Autocrat,* appeared in 1883. A Birthday edition in two volumes was put out in 1891, the same year it became Vol. II of the Riverside edition of the *Writings,* and of the subsequent editions of 1892 and 1893. Only two editions have appeared since Holmes's death in 1894; one in Boston and London, 1902, which ran to four issues; the last, Boston, 1916. An English edition came out the same year as the first book publication here (1860),

making only two; the revised edition, in two volumes, came out in Edinburgh in 1883.

8. When *The Poet* came out as a book in 1872, the subtitle emphasized the supposed single reader: "His [changed in 1883 to *He*] talks with his Fellow-Boarders and the Reader." The London edition, in 1872, omitted the subtitle, but noted the author was the author of *The Autocrat*. Editions followed the pattern of *The Professor*: a revised edition, 1883; a two-volume Edinburgh edition, 1884; the Birthday, 1890; the three in the collected *Writings* of 1891, 1892, and 1893; an edition in Boston and London, 1902; in Boston, 1916. Sales were also about the same; the marked difference was between them and *The Autocrat*, which has sold about twice as many copies as any other of Holmes's works.

9. That Holmes worked hard over "Wind-Clouds and Star-Drifts" (pp. 171-84) as central to the problem he was treating in *The Poet*, is proven by the changes he made when it was published in editions of his poems. He shortened the sections, making twelve instead of seven, and gave each a title. From "Ambition," the progress of the young scientist was marked by "Regrets," "Sympathies," the comfort of "Master and Scholar" to the isolation of "Alone"; he proceeded to brave "Questioning" and "Worship" (a significant juxtaposition); achieved "Manhood" with its "Rights" and "Truths"; but was tempted by "Idols" until finally rescued by "Love." Middle sections were rearranged and sharpened by rewriting some lines and omitting many. Indicative not only of how real to Holmes was the problem of the young scientist but also of how natural to his poetic expression were rhyme and stanza, especially the rhyming couplet for long poems, are the effort, revision, and ultimate failure of this venture into blank verse. I note these changes because they reveal Holmes's special poetic taste and gift; also because it is one of the few instances where textual changes are not carefully recorded in *Bibliog*.

Chapter Four

1. This address was published in Boston and London in February, 1871, "With Notes and Afterthoughts." The attractive format of both books tells of the wide and cultivated audience Holmes had won on both sides of the Atlantic as well as of an awakening interest in approaching the human mind physiologically and analytically. Both editions are printed in large type, that the many examples and references added in footnotes may be readily legible; both have author and title in decorative gilt on the cover as well as on the back. The English edition is more attractive, with wider pages and spaces between lines, and with Holmes's full name spaced by itself

on the cover, as compared to the crowded name with only initials
under huge capitals for the first word of the title on the American
edition. Both carry on the title-page the quotation from Pascal's
Pensées, XI, 4: "Car il ne faut pas se méconnaître, nous sommes
automates autant qu'esprit." The first Boston issue of 1,500 copies
was sold out in March, and a second printed that month; there were
six issues to 1889.

2. A continuing interest in *Elsie Venner,* with its haunting heroine,
is shown by a dramatization under the same title by George H.
Miles, performed in Boston in May, 1865, with one of America's leading
emotional actresses, Mrs. D. P. Bowers, playing the title role. It was
not successful and was soon withdrawn; Holmes, who went to see it
one night from the back of a box, complained: "It was not my Elsie
Venner. They had made it into a melodrama, and the psychology
was not there" (Morse, I, 257). A London edition appeared the same
year as the Boston, 1861, and a French translation in 1862, by
E. D. Forgues, entitled *La sorcière à l'ambre.* It was an abridgment,
one of a series under the heading "Imitations de l'anglais." Besides
the revised edition in 1883, and the three editions of collected works
of 1891, 1892, and 1893, which included all three novels, it was
brought out twice in the Riverside Paper series: as No. 4 in 1885,
as No. 14 in 1890. In 1903, it was one of the Cambridge Classics,
and in 1961, its centennial year, it was one of the New American
Library of World Literature's Signet Classics.

3. Although *The Guardian Angel* was brought out in London the
same month as in Boston—November, 1867—there has been only one
printing besides that for collected *Writings* of 1891, 1892, 1893.
The Riverside Paper series brought it out in 1886 as No. 19, later
as No. 8.

4. So wide was Holmes's circle of readers that there were ten
impressions of *A Mortal Antipathy* as it was brought out in November,
1885, again in time for the Christmas trade. Copies were sent to
London in 1885, 1886, and 1890, but there was no separate edition
there and none there afterwards save in the collected *Writings* of
1891, 1892, 1893.

5. Clarence P. Oberndorf, *The Psychiatric Novels of Oliver
Wendell Holmes* (N.Y. [1943]), pp. vi, 19. The late Dr. Oberndorf
was Clinical Professor of Psychiatry at Columbia University, and his
book was first published by the Columbia University Press in 1943.
A second edition, revised and enlarged to include corrections and
additions sent in by colleagues, was brought out in 1946.

6. That the method Holmes used of collecting and studying
minutiae from which to draw deductions was admired and imitated
by Dr. A. Conan Doyle so consciously that he therefore named his

character who "had a turn for observation and deduction" Sherlock Holmes, is a rumor often mentioned by doctors and returning Rhodes scholars. The only name which may surely be connected with this assertion is the late Christopher Morley's—a name of authority in regard to Sherlock Holmes.

Chapter Five

1. The a.l.s. Holmes to Dr. John Peters, Jan. 8 and Dec. 17, 1859, are in the Peters Scrapbook in the Henry W. and Albert A. Berg Collection of the New York Public Library, and are used here with the permission of Business Manager George L. Schaefer.

The a.l.s. Holmes to Dr. Peters, Dec. 15, 1859, is in Houghton Library, Harvard, and is used here with the permission of Director William A. Jackson.

2. The a.l.s. Holmes to Fields, Dec. 5, 1879, and the clipping with identification cut off, are the property of the Rosenbach Foundation, Philadelphia, and are used here with the permission of Director William McCarthy.

3. For a helpful analysis of Holmes's handling of Emerson's poetic achievement, see Tilton, pp. 347-49.

4. "Order of Services at the Two Hundred and Fiftieth Anniversary of the Organization of the First Church in Cambridge, under Thomas Shepherd, February 1-11, 1636. Friday, February 12, 1886." Holmes took pains that both his father's hymn and his own should be printed in the old style, with all nouns capitalized.

5. Oxford has not yet forgotten the Autocrat: in the *Oxford Magazine* for February, 1949, the article "The Autocrat Visits Oxford" offers comments he might make on contemporary affairs; in the same magazine for March, 1957, "A Chat With The Autocrat" takes up most of the number and continues the parody. Besides witty comments on recent scientific gadgets, Holmes's absorption in and curiosity about natural monstrosities is elaborated. He had a small boy's curiosity about the odd, and Barnum always sent him complimentary tickets when he brought his new sideshows and dancing horses to Boston.

6. This successful cartoon of the rather pompous little Autocrat in tail-coat has been widely circulated. As recently as 1937, a colored enlargement was sent around to American doctors to advertise a new anaesthetic.

Chapter Six

1. *Wellesley Courant*, Dec. 12, 1884.

2. Francis Biddle, *Mr. Justice Holmes* (New York, 1943), p. 62. Quoted from Holmes's Preface to his *Collected Legal Papers*.

3. One of these official notices is in the Clifton Waller Barrett Collection in the Alderman Library of the University of Virginia; it is quoted here with the permission of Mr. Barrett.

4. This a.l.s. of Judge Holmes to Samuel May, Oct. 8, 1894, is in the Classbook of 1829 in the Harvard Archives; it is quoted here with the permission of Custodian Clifford K. Shipton.

Selected Bibliography

PRIMARY SOURCES

A. *The Writings of Oliver Wendell Holmes*. Riverside ed. 13 vols. Boston: Houghton, Mifflin and Co., 1891.
    I. *The Autocrat of the Breakfast-Table*, 1858 (dates after titles are of first book publication)
    II. *The Professor at the Breakfast-Table*, 1860
    III. *The Poet at the Breakfast-Table*, 1872
    IV. *Over the Teacups*, 1891
    V. *Elsie Venner*, 1861
    VI. *The Guardian Angel*, 1867
    VII. *A Mortal Antipathy*, 1885
    VIII. *Pages from An Old Volume of Life: A Collection of Essays*, 1857-1881, 1883
    IX. *Medical Essays 1842-1882*, 1883
    X. *Our Hundred Days in Europe*, 1887
    XI-XIII. *The Poetical Works*
The Complete Poetical Works of Oliver Wendell Holmes, ed. Horace E. Scudder. Cambridge ed. Boston: Houghton Mifflin Co. [cpt. 1908].
Soundings from the Atlantic. Boston: Ticknor & Fields, 1864.
John Lothrop Motley. Boston: Houghton, Osgood & Co., 1878.
Ralph Waldo Emerson. American Men of Letters series. Boston: Houghton, Mifflin and Co., 1885.

B. Dr. Holmes's Contributions to the *Atlantic Monthly*, 1857-1894.
    I. Nov. 1857-May, 1858:
        "The Autocrat of the Breakfast-Table" (Nov.-May)
        "The Homœopathic Domestic Physician" (review, Dec.)
        "Agassiz's Natural History" (review, Jan.)
        "Parthenia" (review, Feb.)
    II. June-Dec., 1858:
        "The Autocrat of the Breakfast-Table" (June-Oct.)
        "Dr. Asa Gray's Botanical Series" (review, Aug.)
        "A Visit to the Autocrat's Landlady" (Nov.)
        "Brief Expositions of Rational Medicine" (review, Nov.)
        "The Last Look" (poem, Nov.)
        "The Autocrat gives a Breakfast to the Public" (Dec.)

III. Jan.-June, 1859:
"The Professor at the Breakfast-Table" (Jan.-June)
"Mothers and Infants, Nurses and Nursing" (review, May)
"The Stereoscope and the Stereograph" (June)

IV. July-Dec., 1859:
"The Professor at the Breakfast-Table" (July-Dec.)
"Love" (review, Sept.)

V. Jan.-June, 1860:
"The Professor's Story [Elsie Venner]" (Jan.-June)
"The Undergraduate" (review, Mar.)

VI. July-Dec., 1860:
"The Professor's Story [Elsie Venner]" (July-Dec.)

VII. Jan.-June, 1861:
"The Professor's Story [Elsie Venner]" (Jan.-April)
"A Visit to the Asylum for Aged and Decaying Punsters" (Jan.)
"Brother Jonathan's Lament for Sister Caroline" (poem, May)
"Army Hymn" (poem, June)

VIII. July-Dec., 1861:
"Sun Painting and Sun Sculpture" (July)
"Parting Hymn" (poem, Aug.)
"Bread and the Newspaper" (Sept.)
"The Wormwood Cordial of History" (Oct.)
"The Flower of Liberty" (poem, Nov.)
"Union and Liberty" (poem, Dec.)

IX. Jan.-June, 1862:
"Voyage of the Good Ship Union" (poem, Mar.)

X. July-Dec., 1862:
"The Poet to His Readers" (poem, July)
"My Hunt After 'The Captain'" (Dec.)

XI. Jan.-June, 1863:
"Choose Ye This Day Whom Ye Will Serve" (poem, Mar.)
"The Human Wheel, its Spokes and Felloes" (May)

XII. July-Dec., 1863:
"Doings of the Sunbeam" (July)
"The Great Instrument" (Nov.)

XIII. Jan.-June, 1864:
"The Minister Plenipotentiary [Mem. tribute to Henry Ward Beecher]" (Jan.)
"The Last Charge" (poem, Feb.)
"Our Classmate [Frederick William Crocker]" (poem, Mar.)

"Our Progressive Independence" (April)
"Shakespeare" (poem, June)
XIV. July.-Dec., 1864:
"Hawthorne" (July)
"In Memory of J. W. — R. W. [John and Robert Ware]"
(poem, July)
"Bryant's Seventieth Birthday" (poem, Dec.)
XV. Jan.-June, 1865:
"God Save the Flag" (poem, Jan.)
"Our Oldest Friend" (poem, Mar.)
"Our First Citizen" [later titled "Edward Everett"]
(poem, April)
"Our Battle Laureate [Henry Howard Brownell]" (May)
XVI. July-Dec., 1865:
"No Time Like the Old Time" (poem, Oct.)
"A Farewell to Agassiz" (poem, Nov.)
XVII. Jan.-June, 1866:
"My Annual" (poem, April)
XIX. Jan.-June, 1867:
"The Guardian Angel" (Jan.-June)
"All Here" (poem, Mar.)
XX. July-Dec., 1867:
"The Guardian Angel" (July-Dec.)
"Chanson Without Music" (poem, Nov.)
XXI. Jan.-June, 1868:
"Once More" (poem, April)
XXII. July-Dec., 1868:
"Bill and Joe" (poem, Sept.)
XXIII. Jan.-June, 1869:
"Cinders From the Ashes" (Jan.)
XXIV. July-Dec., 1869:
"Bonaparte, August 15, 1769—Humboldt, September 14,
1769" (poem, Nov.)
XXV. Jan.-June, 1870:
"Nearing the Snow-Line" (poem, Jan.)
"Even-Song" (poem, Mar.)
XXVII. Jan.-June, 1871:
"Dorothy Q., A Family Portrait" (poem, Jan.)
XXVIII. July-Dec., 1871:
"Life of Major John André" (review, July)
XXIX. Jan.-June, 1872:
"The Poet at the Breakfast-Table" (Jan.-June)
XXX. July-Dec., 1872:
"The Poet at the Breakfast-Table" (July-Dec.)

XXXI. Jan.-June, 1873:
    "After the Fire" (poem, Jan.)
XXXII. July-Dec., 1874:
    "The Fountain of Youth" (poem, Aug.)
    "A Poem Served to Order" (poem, Sept.)
    "Sex in Education" (review, Dec.)
XXXIII. Jan.-June, 1874:
    "An Old-Year Song" (poem, Jan.)
    "A Ballad of the Boston Tea-Party" (poem, Feb.)
XXXIV. July-Dec. 1874:
    "Professor Jeffries Wyman" (Nov.)
XXXV. Jan.-June, 1875:
    "The Americanized European" (review-essay, Jan.)
    "Crime and Automatism" (April)
XXXVI. July-Dec., 1875:
    "Old Cambridge" (poem, Aug.)
    "Exotics" (review, Sept.)
XXXVII. Jan.-June, 1876:
    "A Familiar Letter to Several Correspondents" (poem, Jan.)
    " 'Ad Amicos' " (poem, Mar.)
    "A Memorial Tribute [to Dr. Samuel G. Howe]" (poem, April)
XXXVIII. July-Dec., 1876:
    "How the Old Horse Won the Bet" (poem, July)
XXXIX. Jan.-June, 1877:
    "How Not To Settle It" (poem, Feb.)
    "The First Fan" (poem, June)
XLI. Jan.-June, 1878:
    "My Aviary" (poem, Jan.)
XLII. July-Dec., 1878:
    "The Silent Melody" (poem, Sept.)
XLIV. July-Dec., 1879:
    "Vestigia Quinque Retrorsum" (poem, Aug.)
XLV. Jan.-June, 1880:
    "The Coming Era" (poem, Jan.)
    "The Iron Gate" (poem, Supplement)
    "Dr. Holmes's Reminiscence" (Supplement)
XLVI. July-Dec., 1880:
    "The Archbishop and Gil Blas" (poem, Aug.)
    "Benjamin Peirce: Astronomer, Mathematician 1809-1880" (poem, Dec.)
XLVII. Jan.-June, 1881:
    "Boston to Florence" (poem, Mar.)

XLVIII. July-Dec., 1881:
    "Post Prandial" (poem, Sept.)
XLIX. Jan.-June, 1882:
    "Before the Curfew" (poem, Mar.)
    "Our Dead Singer: H. W. L. [Henry Wadsworth Long-
    fellow]" (poem, June)
L. July-Dec., 1882:
    "At the Summit [Harriet Beecher Stowe's 70th birth-
    day]" (poem, Aug.)
LI. Jan.-June, 1883:
    "An After-Breakfast Talk" (Jan.)
    "A Loving-Cup Song" (poem, Mar.)
    "Pillow-Smoothing Authors" (April)
    "The Flaneur" (poem, May)
LII. July-Dec., 1883:
    "King's Chapel" (poem, Sept.)
LIII. Jan.-June, 1884:
    "At the Saturday Club" (poem, Jan.)
    "The Girdle of Friendship" (poem, Mar.)
    "Thomas Gold Appleton" (June)
LIV. July-Dec., 1884:
    "Ave" (poem, Oct.)
LV. Jan.-June, 1885:
    "The New Portfolio: A Mortal Antipathy" (Jan.-June)
LVI. July-Dec., 1885:
    "The New Portfolio: A Mortal Antipathy" (July-Dec.)
    "Two Anniversary After-Dinner Poems" (Aug.)
LVII. Jan.-June, 1886:
    "The New Portfolio: A Cry from the Study" (Jan.)
    "The New Portfolio: Two Occasional Poems with an
    Interlude" (Mar.)
LVIII. July-Dec., 1886:
    "The New Portfolio: A Prospective Visit" (July)
    "Poem on the Two Hundred and Fiftieth Anniversary of
    the Foundation of Harvard University" (Supplement)
LIX. Jan.-June, 1887:
    "Our Hundred Days in Europe" (Mar.-June)
LX. July-Dec., 1887:
    "Our Hundred Days in Europe" (July-Oct.)
LXI. Jan.-June, 1888:
    "After 'Our Hundred Days'" (Jan.)
    "Over the Teacups" (March)
LXIII. Jan.-June, 1889:
    "To James Russell Lowell [at dinner on 70th birthday]"
    (poem, April)

LXV. Jan.-June, 1890:
    "Over the Teacups" (Jan.-June)
LXVI. July-Dec., 1890:
    "Over the Teacups" (July-Nov.)
    "But One Talent" (poem, Dec.)
LXVIII. July-Dec., 1891:
    "James Russell Lowell" (poem, Oct.)
LXX. July-Dec., 1892:
    "In Memory of John Greenleaf Whittier" (poem, Nov.)
LXXIII. Jan.-June, 1894:
    "Francis Parkman" (poem, Feb.)

SECONDARY SOURCES

CROTHERS, SAMUEL MCCHORD. *Oliver Wendell Holmes: The Autocrat and His Fellow-Boarders.* Boston: Houghton, Mifflin and Co., 1909. A readable essay combines informed appreciation of Holmes's literary craft with emphasis on his penetrating analysis of human tensions and eccentricities.

CURRIER, FRANKLIN T., ed. Eleanor M. Tilton. *A Bibliography of Oliver Wendell Holmes.* New York: New York University Press, 1953. A definitive bibliography, this reports many facts concerning nineteenth-century publishing practices and payments. Full listings and collations are often made significant by supplementary information.

HOLMES, JOHN. *Letters to James Russell Lowell and Others,* ed. William Roscoe Thayer. Introd. Alice M. Longfellow. Boston: Houghton Mifflin Co., 1917. Letters and editorial comment give information about the Holmes family and provide glimpses of the Holmes who was not part of the public image.

HOWE, MARK ANTHONY DEWOLFE. *Holmes of the Breakfast-Table.* New York: Oxford University Press, 1939. A graceful appreciation is made intimate by frequent quotations from Holmes's personal notes to James and Annie Fields.

MORSE, JOHN TORREY, JR. *Life and Letters of Oliver Wendell Holmes.* 2 vols. Boston: Houghton, Mifflin and Co., 1896. A family biography conventional in the nineteenth century; lacking in straightforward chronology and in objective evaluation and analysis, it is nevertheless invaluable for many intimate details which are to be found only in its pages.

OBERNDORF, CLARENCE P. *The Psychiatric Novels of Oliver Wendell Holmes.* New York: Columbia University Press, 1943. A professional psychiatrist's overemphasis on Holmes's anticipation of many of Freud's and Jung's diagnoses does not prevent this book from offering welcome information to the modern reader.

TILTON, ELEANOR M. *Amiable Autocrat: A Biography of Oliver Wendell Holmes.* New York: Henry Schuman, 1947. This carefully documented investigation of Holmes's medical activities gives information about the medical world he joined and the part he played in it. His lecture tours and subjects are recorded in detail.

Index